GAMIFY EDUCATION:

Motivating Students in an Era of Apathy

by

Christopher Becker

and

Jamey Lamberson

Published by Gamify Education LLC
100 N. Howard Street, Suite 4791, Spokane, Washington 99201

Copyright © 2023 Gamify Education LLC

Printed in the United States of America
ISBN: 978-1-962239-00-4

DEDICATION

CB: To my wife, I wouldn't be who I am without you.

JL: To Kadi, my wife, the love of my life.

CONTENTS

PREFACE

In the *Matrix* trilogy, two characters are credited with the design and upkeep of the Matrix, a computer-simulated world designed to contain the minds of humans whose bodies are being used as batteries by their machine overlords. Their names are the Architect and the Oracle.

The Architect is the designer of the program. He makes the sound of a crow cawing, the savory taste of a buttery steak, and the warmth of the sun seem so real that humans don't know they are living in a simulation. In his first iteration of the Matrix, the Architect created a perfect world for humans. The program, however, ultimately failed. Another artificial intelligence was created to help solve the problem. This AI was called the Oracle.

The Oracle's job was to get humans to accept the program by making the world relatable so that everyone went along with their lives. She did this by creating choice and chaos.

My teaching partner, Mr. Becker, is the Architect. I, Mr. Lamberson, am the Oracle.

This is Mr. Becker. If you haven't figured it out, my words are written in unbolded text. Mr. Lamberson's words, true to his personality, are written in bolded text. In this book, we will be speaking fluent "Teacherese". We will use words and jargon that teachers use. We won't care about starting sentences with "and" or even worry about writing sentences at all. We hope this way of writing will sound more relatable to you. That's what we want: to simply have a conversation about a very transformative practice.

Are you ready to join the revolution of rethinking and reshaping *motivational play* in education?

Mr. Lamberson and I believe that the current educational system needs to change. Too many students are not being helped. Too many kids are not inspired. Too many children are not motivated at school. This book is the first step in what hopefully brings gigantic reform to our profession. We have embarked on a startup company called Gamify Education. Our mission is to empower teachers so that all students can become the best versions of themselves.

This is not a book about using a bunch of different educational games in your classroom. It is so much more than that. This book is all about how a teacher can transform the classroom into a game itself. Through it, students will be motivated to learn. They will embrace a sense of belonging, and more than likely, enjoy school more.

Here's the best part: teachers can keep doing what they've always been doing! They can–and should–use the same books, the same math manipulatives, the same science experiments, and the same novels. The Game is simply a platform from which the instructor can teach. It is always at the forefront, but at the same time, hidden in the shadows.

We believe so much in the power of *motivational play* that by the end of this book, we will give you a blueprint for a very simple, yet incredibly fun classroom game. Hopefully, this will alleviate some pressure if you are thinking that designing a classroom game is too big of an undertaking.

Before you read on, imagine the end of the school year in which you say to yourself:

"What just happened? How could a simple classroom game do all this?"

Is it magic? Hardly. This book will simply help teachers unleash the power behind what every child wants…

To simply play.

C.B. and J.L.

CHAPTER 1:
THE ORIGIN STORY

Teacher, welcome to The Game. I don't want to alarm you, but this is a high-stakes game we are playing. Lives are at stake, and I'm not talking about how many more tries Mario has to save the princess. You are playing for the future lives of the students in your classroom. This year, you have the potential to be the greatest indicator of success for them. But as good as this sounds, you also could be blamed for the lack of it. I told you the stakes were high. But enough of the things you already probably know. Let's get started.

I would like to think you picked up this book because you are looking for a new and innovative way to motivate a generation with short-attention spans, a fixation on video games, and an addiction to social media. It's a generation who can scroll for hours but, at the same time, fail to do ten minutes of a reading assignment. I hope you are the teacher who still has that innate desire to change lives.

But this might not be you. You might be more disillusioned than that. You might be at your wit's end, and this is your Hail Mary. You might even be the teacher who just joined the book study to get extra pay. I'm not judging. I've been there.

You might be open to having a game drive your educational practices and decisions, or this might terrify you. You may believe it could work, or you might be on the other side. You might be the individual thinking:

"Education should have value in itself, and creating a game only cheapens it."

Thank you for playing so far.

Hello, Mr. Lamberson here. I am much more blunt than my good friend, Mr. Becker. There are only two reasons you would be reading this book. Either you are being forced to, or you are already an awesome teacher who is constantly looking to improve your practice.

If you are the latter, then good for you. Pat yourself on the back. You're awesome. I think you are really going to enjoy this book. If you are the former, I beg you to have an open mind to the concepts we are presenting.

In this world there are two types: doers and excuse makers. The world of education is no different and has both. Excuse makers always have a reason that their classes are failing:

"Oh, if only you taught at MY school. You don't know MY kids."

I have taught at YOUR school. Actually, I AM teaching at your school, a Title I school where over 80% of the students qualify for free/reduced lunch. It's a place where roughly fifteen different languages are spoken. It has a large monolingual population from all over the spoken spectrum—from Burmese to Arabic and everything in between.

Also, I do know YOUR kids. These are students who go home to parents who are so stressed out about life that they can't even process the idea of pushing their child to be successful

academically. Your students are real kids with real trauma and real deficits. These are the individuals we have been called to help and educate.

You might be wondering who we are.

In order to answer that, let's back up nine years. As the newly minted math coach/specialist in my school, I wound up working with our district's head of curriculum for math and science. Her name was Kathy Fisk, God rest her soul. She was one of the most genuine and delightful individuals who I have had the pleasure of working with.

Kathy planned our professional development (PD) for the district. The trip she was especially fond of was a week in Las Vegas for a Singapore Math seminar. I honestly didn't know much about Singapore or why I would want to learn its math at the time, but when Kathy asked, I agreed to go.

To save money, the district always books a hotel room with two beds for two teachers. When going over the travel logistics, someone at the district told me my roommate was a teacher from another school—some guy named Chris Becker.

"Okay," I thought, a touch sarcastically. "Guess I'm making a new friend." Little did I know just a handful of years later, my wife and I would be the godparents of their youngest daughter.

Life is funny that way.

Around the same time, I was also told by the district I would be sharing a room with another teacher. The name I got was Jamey Lamberson. I had no idea who this person was or what grade this teacher taught, but I did know the school. I did a little digging. On the school website, I clicked on "Staff List" and immediately saw the picture of a woman with the caption, "Mrs. Lamberson, Kindergarten Teacher."

Oh, no.

I was brand new to public education, but I was surprised that the district would pair up a male and female teacher to share a hotel room. Maybe *that* was why my parents sent me to private school my whole life.

"My wife wouldn't let me room with another woman," the voice in my head told me. "Or would she?"

After my wife showed me my error, I emailed Kathy saying that I wouldn't be able to go to this incredible math conference because I couldn't room with a woman. I later got Kathy's response:

"Christopher!!! Jamey's a guy!"

Apparently, there were *two* Lambersons teaching at that school. Mrs. Lamberson taught kindergarten while Mr. Lamberson was the math specialist. If only their school would have put the picture of the math specialist before the pictures of the kindergarten teachers on their school's website…

…that would have saved me from the wrath of an unhappy wife.

✳✳✳✳✳✳✳✳✳✳

Man, does Vegas do a good job of selling itself. I really thought that I was going to enjoy that place. I did not.

We got to Vegas and found our hotel. After checking in and unpacking, we headed out for a bite to eat. Because the crowds were so stupidly massive, we basically had to walk single file at a snail's pace. Standing in a line of people when it's dark and hot trying to find the TGI Friday's is not my idea of a good time.

Back at the hotel, it became apparent that my roomie also wasn't impressed by the situation. Instead of going back out on The Strip, I found the deck of cards I had stashed in my bag. I

held it up and asked my roommate, "Do you like games?"

Oh boy, little did I know.

CHAPTER 2:
THE MOMENT OF TRUTH

Covid-19 brought a lot of tragedy to a lot of families. There is no denying that, and I don't want to downplay any of it. For teachers, though, I think it made us appreciate what we get to do on a daily basis in a non-pandemic school year. This is all to say that teaching during the Covid-19 pandemic was the hardest year of teaching in my fifteen-year career.

We didn't get to start the year with any students sitting in their seats. Teaching was to be done through video conference calls with time set aside for the students to work. I suppose this was better than at the end of the 2019-2020 school year when schools shut down with no plan in place.

At least we had a plan. It wasn't a great plan by any means, but the education leaders insisted that students would learn the same amount during the remote (and eventually hybrid days) as if they were sitting at their desks in the actual school building.

Yeah, right.

I, as a teacher, couldn't even (technically? legally?) tell my students to turn on their cameras for reasons of equity. So, for six weeks or so, I was teaching five dedicated faces, two dedicated-but-extremely-pixelated faces, and about six black screens with muted microphones. And yes, I had way more than thirteen students.

I don't have nearly as good of stories as the Internet, but I watched students try to learn with shirtless little brothers jumping all over them. Students were trying to respond to questions while sitting in a noisy gymnasium called a study center, or my personal favorite, one of my students was caught binge watching *Stranger Things* as I was attempting to teach.

School districts adopted many different types of instructional models during the pandemic. Hindsight is 20/20, but most of them sucked. I'm not here to critique any particular approach, but our district tried the best they could with the restrictions they got. We did not stay fully "remote" for very long in our district. Thank God, too, because remote was the worst.

Things got a little better later in the year when a thing called hybrid learning was put in place. Students could come back to the building, but they had to remain six feet apart. The only way this would work was if there were two sets of kids: the A and the B students. Group A would meet on Mondays and Tuesdays. Wednesdays were set aside for asynchronous planning on the part of the teachers. The B students would attend school on Thursdays and Fridays.

Over the course of the next six weeks or so, I got extremely frustrated with most of my students not doing any of the asynchronous work that I assigned them to do. The five-day weekend was a real thing for them. Most of my students lacked any drive or purpose to enhance their learning. I–along with every other teacher in America–was struggling to motivate these young people to complete their assignments.

I tried convincing them with logical arguments. I explained to

8

them that in a normal year with five days being at school, it was still incredibly difficult to master all the fifth-grade standards. Since they were only at school two days a week, they needed to work extremely hard on the days they weren't there.

That didn't work.

I tried "fussing" at them. You know, that great word that Atlanta-based educator Ron Clark may or may not have coined. It is really the same as yelling at the students; but it's not yelling, it's just fussin' at them.

I was going to bribe them with candy, but, apparently, that was against Covid-19 protocols. It was at this time I threw my hands in the air with no more words left and no new ideas to try.

I, on the other hand, had resigned myself to the new reality and had taken the it-is-what-it-is mentality. Since everyone had the same problem, I figured it wasn't *my* problem. I have a life philosophy that if I don't have the power to change something, then I shouldn't concern myself with thought nor effort to fix that thing. In this instance, I truly believed that there wasn't anything I could do to help motivate my students beyond badgering. Boy, am I glad I teach with Mr. Becker. When he gets something stuck in his craw, he's like a Pit Bull with a T-bone. You have a better chance of getting struck by lightning than you do of him letting it go.

Call it "fate" or "divine intervention", but a new idea came in an email one winter afternoon. One perk of passing the National Boards for the Certification of Teaching **[flex]** is they send you a near-daily email about the teaching profession. I read very few of them, but if a title is intriguing enough, I will click on it.

Now, please forgive me. I don't remember the exact article that I clicked on, but I do know it dealt with a teacher out East using game-like elements in his classroom. This sparked my interest. I immediately started to research this idea. I envisioned how I could motivate my students with game mechanics. I was floating high, convinced that this idea was going to be exactly what my students and I needed.

Truth be told, I was neck high in a home remodel project which was a great distraction from the bleak reality of teaching during a pandemic. Then, one February morning, Mr. Becker walked into my classroom and said, "I've got an idea."

To which I replied, "Okay, hit me with it."

You see, whenever Mr. Becker has an idea, it means that he is looking to radically and fundamentally change our practice. The last time he had an idea, we spent two years designing an ELA curriculum.

With that look in his eyes, he told me, "I've got an idea…" AND he followed with, "…this is going to be big."

I began to get nervous. His last idea wasn't big, and it consumed our planning for two years.

"I want to transform my classroom into a giant game, and I think all of fifth grade should do it."

✱✱✱✱✱✱✱✱✱✱

Have you ever told your students to write a story, and they say, "What do I write about?"

"Whatever you want!" you exclaim.

And then the child sits there, staring at his blank page hoping that some idea would pop into his head. That was me in February of 2021. I was fired up to try and motivate my students with a game, but I felt deflated that I didn't have a good plan in place. I read more articles and even a book about using gamification elements in education. But even after all that research, I didn't feel like I could do it. I just had a ton of abstract ideas with a giant blank page in front of me. Frustrated, I figured I had two options:

#1) I could give up, but then I would be left with no other ideas on how I could motivate my students during a hybrid teaching year in the middle of a global pandemic.

#2) I could somehow work through my frustration to see if I couldn't figure out what was missing.

There was actually a third option: bring your frustration to the team and hash out the ideas together.

Mr. Becker and I work really well as a team, but it's not because we always agree. In fact, we almost never agree on anything initially. It often takes hours of speaking loudly to each other and drawing doodles on the whiteboard to come to an agreement on anything. Anyone who doesn't know us might think we hate each other as we are working through concepts.

We don't try to win the conversation. We try to figure out the best solution. That's the magic. If you are a lone wolf and you want to transform your classroom, you will absolutely be able to do it using the principles we outline in the later chapters. But if do you have a partner (or team) who is willing to embark on this journey with you, then you will end up better because of it.

Mr. Lamberson encouraged me not to abandon this radical idea, and we eventually figured it out. But as I reflect on that time, the thing that caused me so much frustration is also the thing that so many people have wrong about gamifying education.

Elements of gamification have been around for decades, and many people and companies have found success using them. Leaderboards, streak bonuses, gems, levels, and other rewards are just a few things you might notice on a productivity or learning app that uses gaming elements. These tend to be the same things associated with gamifying a classroom.

I think there is a problem with this, though. Many people simply complete these tasks, thereby gaining extrinsic rewards. But when the rewards are taken away or start to get old, the motivation stops and so does the desired result. Even worse, though, is the fear of losing something you earned, especially when there is a streak involved.

Every day, my wife plays a game on her phone that involves connecting a bunch of colored dots to the dot of the same color. As of writing this book, she has played this game for an ultra-impressive 2,000 straight days. Every day, I "learn" Spanish on my phone via an app. I have done this for 1,700 straight days. How do I know? The app tells me. Why do I keep plugging away at learning Spanish? It's simple. I don't want my streak to end. If I forgot to practice Spanish or if I had to create a new account, my streak would go from a glorious 1,700 to a dismal 0. If that happened, I am certain that I would not open that Spanish app again for a long time.

Maybe even ever.

A few years ago, the Lambersons and the Beckers drove to Portland to see a concert. Before the show, we arrived at a restaurant to have dinner. We were having a delightful evening, eating good food and sharing laughs when suddenly Mr. Becker shouted, "Oh, no, my streak!"

He then proceeded to pull out his phone in that noisy restaurant to complete his Spanish lesson.

The fear is real.

****

At the end of February of 2021, I finally had the aha moment that was needed. I realized that I was trying to attach all of these ideas of play without the play itself. It was almost like getting a bunch of people together next to a basketball hoop with a ball in hand. The teams get formed, and you say, "Okay, that was fun. Let's go home."

This is why simply using gamification elements in a classroom isn't that powerful. The play is missing. Teachers, this is the secret to unlock student motivation in our current era of apathy.

Looking back, it seems very easy to see. Doesn't the answer to using elements of gamification always point back to The Game itself? Without it, what does it point to?

Nothing.

The classroom leaderboard will simply be a ranking of your students. The gold that students can earn will eventually be exchanged for a dollar store prize. Your students will eventually realize the shortcomings. They will see that the leaderboard is just a list of the Top 10 "smartest" kids in class. And all that gold? Well, after the first pencil broke, they might not be that motivated to earn another one. Then what?

You better keep learning, or else…your 35-day streak of recess will be reset to zero.

****

I still remember telling my mom my new idea of creating The Game. Her first question was, "What will the kids learn?"

"Nothing," I told her. She was wondering what math or ELA standards would be hit. Do you know the look some people give when they think you have a really bad idea? That was the look my mother gave me.

I don't blame my mom for her reaction at all. She was thinking that The Game was going to center on something specific, like creating equivalent fractions for a math lesson. Although there can be great power in standard-specific games, implementing a classroom game can be exponentially more impactful.

"How so?"

Instead of having the play tied to just one or two specific learning targets, the play in my classroom is tied to all of them!

I recently attended my nephew's high school graduation party where I joined the circle of graduates. "Basically," I told these high schoolers, "I turned my classroom into a yearlong RPG." That's all I said. Then the questions started flying:

"So, your kids have...like characters?"

"Yep."

"How do they level up?"

"They earn XP for proving that they have learned a concept."

"So, they get XP for tests and stuff?"

"Yep."

"So, is there...like a map they are playing on?"

"Yep."

"What do they do on the map?"

"They explore, battle each other, and fight monsters."

"No way! That sounds so sick."

"Yup."

"I wish my teachers would have done that. I would have worked so much harder."

Turning your classroom into a giant game isn't going to be something you need to explain to your students. Gamifying your classroom and using *motivational play* is merely translating desired outcomes into the language that they have grown up using. I have yet to have a student confused by The Game. In fact, we often get students who transfer into the school midyear. With very little explanation, they instantly jump in and start performing like they never had before.

The first year I introduced the classroom game to my students, I thought it would be arduous. Frankly, I was shocked by the reaction of my students. Not only did they get it, but they also understood The Game better than I did.

✱✱✱✱✱✱✱✱✱✱

After I realized the play was missing, the next step was trying to figure out how to incorporate the play with an actual game. I first got to work thinking about games that I had played in the past. I thought about card games, video games, and board games. I have roughly 90 of these rather expensive games on a bookshelf in my house. Nearly all the board games I own have something in common. There needs to be a significant level of strategy to it, or else I'll never open the box. As much as I like playing games, I actually don't like playing anything when the level of luck is too high or if I don't have enough control over the outcome. These two "rules" may seem the same and, in some cases, they are. Hear me out, though.

If I had the opportunity to play Steph Curry in basketball, I would initially be excited for the chance to meet him and watch him play. But after he would beat me game after game, shutout after shutout, I would be very frustrated playing this game. I wish I could blame my defeats on luck, but, of course, there is very little luck involved in basketball. I would keep losing because my skill level is far inferior to his. I wouldn't have enough control over the outcome going into the game, so I wouldn't enjoy the competition.

My mother-in-law, whom I unironically adore, introduced me to the game of *Bunko*. I am not going to get into the nitty-gritty details of the game. They don't matter. What you need to know is that it is a game of 100% chance. The only factor you can control in the game is the speed at which you roll the dice.

In *Bunko*, there are multiple prizes handed out for different categories within the "game".

I love that you put game in quotations.

One such prize is given for the most six-of-a-kinds called "Bunkos". Another is for the most losses. Since the only area of the game you can actually control is the speed at which you play, the only victory you can sway away from probability is most losses. At the most basic root, the way to win the game is by having the highest score after rolling the dice. So, if you can let the other players get in front of you and then hold the dice until the round is over, you guarantee losing. That victory prize for most losses at the end of the night will be yours.

My brother and I devised this strategy several years ago at a family Christmas *Bunko* party. People thought we were joking. We were not. It was the first time I had fun playing *Bunko*. Not only was I somewhat in control of my destiny, but I also had competition. We were both competing to lose.

In *Bunko*, you are paired with random partners each round. If they are under the illusion that the game is fun and winnable, they get very upset by my strategy. This bit of added social pressure didn't bother my brother or me because we wanted to win. The only way to guarantee a win was to lose.

You should design an inspirational poster with the quote, "The only way to guarantee a win is to lose."

We don't play *Bunko* much anymore in my family.

Winning the game. Obvious, right? Can you even imagine playing a game in which the foremost goal is not to win? Me either. But my sister can. She even has the audacity to tell me things like, "I don't play games to win."

What?!

She continues, "I play games for the experience."

It's like she is speaking a different language.

"Show me someone who is okay with losing and I will show you a loser." This was the text I received one night from Mr. Becker. He was watching TV and heard this quote from some coach. He was like, "This is going up in my classroom!"

No, no, no…This was a quote from Buffalo Bills quarterback Josh Allen when he was asked what he thought of his offensive coordinator smashing his headset on the counter after a loss. I did say, though, that the quote was going to go up in my room. Then, I told my counselor wife. It never made it up on my wall.

If there are people who play games for the experience, then this was going to be the easy part of transforming the classroom into a giant game. But, for students like Mr. Lamberson and me, experiencing the game wouldn't be enough. We would still want to win it.

Games like *Candyland, Chutes and Ladders*, and *Sorry* seem fun on the surface because there is a lot of movement. But most of the time, if a player follows a set path, it is more like being a spectator watching the story of the game unfold as the whims of probability sweep you to-and-fro.

Poetic, Mr. Lamberson.

The games on my shelf aren't better than the games on your

shelf. The point of us explaining the luck and skill aspect of games is that an overarching classroom game cannot be based on luck. It needs to be based on skill, or else it will never work.

Back in 2021, I thought of the longest board game I had ever played: Mr. Lamberson's favorite game, *Risk*. For those of you who don't know, it's a territory-controlling game that involves attackers and defenders and a lot of dice rolling. I really like that game, and I could envision students getting invested in a game like that.

Even though *Risk* could take six hours, it is nothing compared to some tactical role-playing games (RPGs) I had played on my Nintendo systems. An RPG is like an adventure for the character. A lot of times, the story is driven by a lot of text and turn-based actions. A tactical RPG brings chess-like movements into the story. Ironically enough, one of these tactical RPG games was released about the same time the entire world shut down; needless to say, I had a lot of spare time on my hands. I easily logged 100 hours of gameplay into that RPG.

Remember when I saw how many hours you played when I was playing my own Nintendo Switch? And then you immediately turned off the setting that allowed me to see it?

I thought if I could merge this video game with *Risk*, it would be something that I would thoroughly want to play. If 36-year-old Chris would want to play it, then there was no doubt that 11-year-old Chris would have flipped out if his teacher invited him to play it for the rest of the school year.

With no real understanding of what we were doing and absolutely no idea what we were getting ourselves into, Mr. Lamberson and I pressed the START button.

CHAPTER 3:
AN INWARD HESITATION

I student-taught in a "gifted" fourth grade classroom. My master teacher was an amazing educator from whom I learned so much. I basically just copied her for the first five years of my career, right down to calling out "ladies and gentlemen" to get my class's attention.

For the first two weeks, I just watched her teach, trying to absorb as much as I could. One day, I observed her lesson on the long division algorithm. Instead of just telling the students the necessary steps, she designed the whole thing around spelunking. The students became cave explorers, and each digit of the dividend was a different-sized cave. I sat in amazement as I watched a true master make something as boring as the division algorithm into a magical, cave-exploring adventure.

Part of my program required me to create a reading unit. At my master teacher's request, I used the book *The BFG*. I included everything required by my college. The students would work collaboratively in groups. There were activities for

each chapter. I even attached the necessary standards to that sucker. The time came to submit my work to my master teacher for review.

I sat in silence watching her read this lesson. I thought it was going to be nothing but positive feedback. After she was done reading, she smiled at me and said, "It's a good start, but…"

She finished her critique with three words that have stuck with me for my career and have shaped my entire practice:

"…where's the fun?"

✳✳✳✳✳✳✳✳✳✳

Mr. Lamberson's master teacher had sixteen years of teaching experience. My master teacher was a six-year-old.

One Saturday morning a few years back, my wife asked me to fold the laundry. Folding clothes—especially the sorting part—was not my strong suit. This was especially true when two of my daughters (ages two and four at the time) were both wearing the same-sized clothes. When I asked my wife how I was supposed to know which clothes went to each daughter, her response was, "Don't you know what clothes your child wears?"

I needed help. I recruited my (then) six-year-old, making her leave her playtime with her two younger sisters. We set up three laundry baskets next to a giant mound of wrinkled, almost-freshly-washed clothes.

We were pretty focused on the task at hand for about three minutes. Then I could see the loss of energy fill my daughter's face. I told her that sometimes we just need to do things that we don't really want to do, and she could play with her sisters after we were done. She sighed and got back to work.

I picked up a shirt and attempted to toss it into one of the baskets. It hit off the rim and fell on the carpet. My daughter promptly pointed out that I missed. She then said I wasn't even shooting at the correct basket. She picked up the shirt, took a few steps back, and shot it into the correct hamper. A smile ran across her face. She then proceeded to "shoot" the remaining clothes until all the clothes were sorted.

As I watched this energetic girl finish her chore, I was taken aback at what just happened. Minutes earlier, I was trying to reason with a grumpy child about doing things that weren't fun. Her frown and grumpy attitude remained. But now, as she gave me a high five as she proceeded to take her clothes to her room, a critical question arose. Did my daughter just trick herself into doing something she didn't enjoy?

If you are thinking about gamifying your classroom and are on the fence about it, ask yourself, "Where is the fun in my classroom?" I guarantee that if you give it a real go and set up a classroom game, your students will be lost in the fun. As you see your students having all this fun, I also guarantee that *your* level of fun will increase. You might actually end up having more fun than your students. You are the Gamemaster, after all.

This brings me to an important point. Humans like to play. Humans like to have fun. Our children are humans. They want to have fun.

Let 'em have it.

I am confident that there are some people who do not think work and fun should be mixed. **(These are the same people from *Footloose* who banned dancing.)** So, when we tell teachers to create a fun-filled classroom game, there are undoubtedly skeptics and naysayers. But that's not the only criticism of this approach. For these reasons, we have come up with five arguments—and how to debunk them—about why you shouldn't gamify your classroom. The first argument is a doozy, so the rest of this chapter

21

will be covering that one. The remaining four will be discussed in the chapter that follows.

Argument #1: Students should find the value in learning itself. They should be intrinsically motivated to learn. They shouldn't need all those extrinsic rewards from a classroom game.

By far, this is the argument that will be brought up most when discussing if a teacher or school should gamify education. In its simplest form, this argument hinges on the philosophy behind motivation. The scope of this book is not how motivational research aligns or doesn't align with what we are telling you. We are not expert researchers, but we do consider ourselves to be expert teachers—two teachers who are convinced that *motivational play* has tremendous benefits with very few drawbacks. If an increase in test scores is more your thing, we do have our own data to back up our claims.

Think about one of the most important questions we will ever ask you:

What kind of student says she likes math, or what kind of student says he likes reading?

We're going to answer this question by describing what type of student that person is not. In our combined thirty years in education, Mr. Lamberson and I have rarely—if ever—heard a student say she liked math when she thought she wasn't good at it. On the contrary, the kids who say they like it are almost all the time the kids who are good at it. We have rarely—if ever—heard a student say he liked reading class when he scored in the bottom 20th percentile on the last standardized reading test.

In almost all cases, intrinsic motivation will never exist if there is no success attached to it.

Just so we are on the same page, let's say intrinsic motivation is defined as doing something for the inherent satisfaction you

feel from completing the task.

I tell students all the time that the reason they don't like *xyz* is because it is challenging for them. Nobody inherently likes things that are too hard. When I was a young man, I was allergic to running. In middle school, we would have to run the mile. I made up all kinds of excuses as to why my mile time was just shy of a full class period. I even convinced myself that I had asthma. It turned out that I hated it because I was bad at it. I was chubby, it was hard, and I didn't like it.

This is what your low-performing students are suffering from.

It wasn't until I was much older that I learned to appreciate running. It wasn't because I found some deep satisfaction in the runs themselves. I had kids. I knew that I wanted to be around and healthy for them, so I pushed myself to run. Once I got over my mental barrier, I found that I actually enjoyed running. I became pretty good at it. This led me to trying all kinds of other difficult physical activities including CrossFit and powerlifting. Today, I hate missing workouts because...

I'm going to cut Mr. Lamberson off. I will tell you why. He hates missing workouts because he likes bragging about how much he can lift.

True...but my greater point is that I avoided the thing I was bad at, but I was drawn to music. I had a natural knack for it. I even minored in music in college. I enjoyed it because I got lots of positive attention for my abilities.

I, unlike Mr. Lamberson, have very few musical talents. When I was in fourth grade, I played the recorder. Because I had to. When I was in my teacher-training program, I learned the basics of playing the piano. Once again, because I had to.

Yes. Part of my teacher-training program was a year-long trudge of Keyboarding 1 and Keyboarding 2. Apparently, the fourteen other non-musical kids and I didn't have enough credits in the arts. That was one of my least favorite college classes. Not only did we have to play in front of the class and the teacher, but we also had to practice at night. The only thing that year of keyboarding classes got me was fulfilling all the requirements for becoming a teacher.

Maybe it's not a running or piano story for you, but I am almost positive that you have a similar story. As a teacher, then, how are you going to motivate students to learn something if they don't feel they are good at it? By intrinsically motivating them?

No!

You are not going to motivate students who have a preconception of failure by relying on intrinsic motivation. It won't happen. As a profession then, can we please stop promoting it?

How do we get students to find success in reading, math, writing, or music when they don't view themselves as good enough? You can sit with them one-on-one and push them to work, but you have 20 to 40 some-odd students to manage and not enough time in a school year.

What if there was a different way for students to become the best versions of themselves?

****

Deep down, I think teachers understand that most of their students aren't intrinsically motivated to learn all the things teachers force them to understand. That itself is part of the problem. Students don't have enough autonomy regarding what they want to study. Unfortunately—at least for Mr. Lamberson and me—this is kind of a moot point. We are handcuffed to so many things that we must do. We have state standards, district curriculums, and school mandates. Our performance as a teacher is based on tests administered at the end of the year. Nothing on the educational horizon is going to change any of this. Until there is a massive overhaul at the district, state, and even federal level, the argument of autonomy is rather pointless for teachers like us and for most public-school teachers.

Remember, we are more of the mindset of trying to change the things that we can control. One of these things is how to motivate students to do things they don't intrinsically want to do. These students need an extra push to get started. They need some external factor.

Education is littered with external motivators, and teachers realize the potential power behind them. To prove the saturation of extrinsic motivators in the education system, we have devised a short list:

-Letter grades and percentages
-Percentile ranks on standardized tests
-Class ranks based on grades
-GPA
-Scholarship opportunities
-Eligibility to compete in extracurriculars
-Money for grades
-Positive feedback for being a good student
-Honor Class placement
-Acceptance into college
-"Red days", "yellow days", and "green days"
-Means to get a desired occupation
-Loss of recess/privileges or extra recess/privileges
-Notes or phone calls home about "good" or "bad" days
-Classroom or school stores
-Candy or other rewards given out for good behavior
-Not getting a switch swatted across your knuckles

After reading that long list that isn't even exhaustive, we are hoping that you are questioning the validity of some of these external factors. Some of these motivators don't seem very effective. Some don't seem equitable, and some seem just plain wrong.

One of the worst educational consequences of the COVID shutdown was an erosion of the pull our educational institutions have on students. For time immemorial, teachers and parents have impressed upon students the importance of grades and attendance. When COVID hit, students got a free pass to the next grade level, and schools weren't allowed to inquire about attendance.

I get it. Things weren't equitable. Some students had computers, the Internet, and parents helping them at home. Some students had nothing. I am not arguing that the decisions made were wrong. What I am saying is that many students didn't care about grades and attendance like they used to.

For us, hybrid learning brought back letter grades, but they carried very little weight. My own son, a 90th percentile reader, was assigned phonic work. Instead of wasting his time with things he already knew, my wife and I had him read books at his level. We informed his teacher about the concept of mastery-based grading. She didn't care. She just said that his grade was based on the number of minutes in the phonics program.

He got an F.

Meh. We never even told him about this. What would be the point?

I recently watched *Ferris Bueller's Day Off*. In the movie, Ferris avoids the vice principal because he is in jeopardy of not graduating due to his nine absences for the year. I almost did a spit take. I would kill for a class average of nine absences in this post-COVID era.

The old approach of motivating students isn't working like it used to.

By setting up a classroom game, students will be extrinsically pushed to learn. They will earn rewards for making growth and showing mastery. Their characters will become stronger, and they will feel more successful. Students know they are going to be rewarded when they reach certain milestones or accomplishments. They will work incredibly hard to gain these rewards.

Some people will say that this approach is wrong. They say that if you tell your students that they will earn something if they complete a math worksheet, then those children will never do another math worksheet if they don't have a future reward attached to it.

If that were true, why do most parents use some kind of reward system to potty-train their young children? Candy and stickers can be great motivators to get kids out of diapers, but eventually they won't be needed.

We understand the sentiment, though. That's why we rarely reward students for just completing a task they are expected to complete. We will reward growth and mastery but not sheer fulfillment of something that they are expected to do.

Moreover, the external factors of *motivational play* are different than external motivators not associated with the play itself. Although we can't prove this point definitively, we do have some ideas to why extrinsic factors of *motivational play* are different— and far superior—to those factors of non-play.

Idea #1: Game rewards are priceless within The Game but completely worthless outside of it.

In my earlier years of being a teacher, I would sometimes hand out suckers to students who were working hard or who got a good grade on a test. I still remember when Jimmy didn't do well on his assessment. When he realized he didn't earn his sucker, do you know what he told me?

"Mr. Becker, I can just go buy a giant bag of suckers."

And that's what he did. That very night, he bought a giant bag of the same suckers I had given out that day. The next day at school, he opened his backpack and showed me that he didn't need my suckers anymore.

Now, think about game rewards. If a student could earn a very powerful card in The Game, there is no store that sells it. There is no price tag on it, and frankly, it is worth $0.00 to everyone else who is not playing The Game.

Game rewards are incredibly powerful and absurdly bizarre. We cannot think of any other motivators that compare to it. How can something be of immense value while at the same time having no value at all?

Mr. Becker will often criticize me for being too impulsive and generous with the rewards I give to my class. Something about ruining the balance of the game…blah blah blah. I don't really pay attention.

Our classroom game had different cards the students could buy with their gold. These cards would give them different power-ups: extra attack bonuses, extra defense, extra moves on the map… things like that. The cards were ranked with a star system. A one-star card was junky, and a five-star card could only be gifted by a Gamemaster for some epic achievement.

One day, I was feeling froggy and I thought, "What if I offer a four-star card to my students if they complete this group task?"

I took one of the best cards in our game and put it face down on the board. I told my class, "This is a four-star card."

The room fell silent.

"I am going to put a math challenge problem on the whiteboard. Your job is to make sure everyone in your group knows the answer and can explain how to get the solution. I

**will give you ten minutes. Then, I will randomly choose
a student to share. If that student can explain the answer
correctly, he or she gets the card."**

**Saying the class lost their minds, doesn't do it justice. I then
put the timer on the board and said go. You could have heard
a pin drop for the first five minutes. Then something amazing
happened. All at once, the students began discussing and
sharing their ideas. By the end, a perfectly average student,
who would have never solved the challenging problem on a
normal day, gave a perfect answer and walked away the hero
of the room. His classmates kept whispering, "Let me see it!"
and, "Oh man, you're so lucky."**

**What did it cost me? Literally nothing. It was a piece of paper.
In that moment, though, what was it worth to that young
man?**

The entire world.

****

I am not a big video game player, but I do get into spurts when I
play a few hours of video games every day for weeks on end. One
of these spans came about five years ago with a game I played on
my iPad.

The app was a superhero-based game that involved placing one's
characters on a grid. There were a lot of game elements that got me
hooked. For one, it involved classic superheroes. There was also a
lot of strategy.

Then the players got ranked. There were different levels, and even
a leaderboard for the Top 10 finishers in the world. At the end of
the week, players got rewards based on what tier they landed in. I
don't want to brag or anything, but I finished in the Top 10 in the
world, not once, but twice, in a game you have never heard of and

no longer exists.

With these new rewards, you could open virtual packs of superhero cards. The packs would open, and you would hope for the ultra-rare, most powerful heroes.

But then the gems would run out, and the players would no longer have that rush of hoping to find the most elite cards in the game. Unless of course, they purchased more gems with real US dollars. You see, the download was free, and for some people like me, all those hours of fun had a price tag of exactly $0.00.

I was kind of obsessed about trying to make that Top 10 list, so I joined a group of other players to trade rare cards. It was a virtual collaboration app which allowed chatting with strangers from around the world.

Remember how I said you could use real money to buy gems in the game? Well, one of the players in this group of strangers mentioned one time how he spent some money on these gems. I get it. Ten, twenty bucks, right?

No. He said he spent his rent money.

A couple different things shocked me about this statement. First was the exuberant amount of money that was spent on this fictional, in-game currency. Rent equals hundreds of dollars, maybe even thousands. The other thing that floored me was that an adult was spending this type of money! I could easily understand a nine-year-old with his mom's credit card hitting the "purchase" button over and over again. But an adult?

If a video game of tic-tac-toe superheroes got a grown man to spend hundreds of hours to make a Top 10 list and got other adults to spend thousands of dollars, can we all agree that rewards attached to play are some of the most unique and powerful motivators that exist?

Idea #2: Extrinsic rewards don't really exist when playing a game.

Imagine playing a game where "if-then" statements didn't occur. Don't try too hard because it's impossible. Every single game is made up of these statements. If a five is rolled, then the player gets to move five spaces. If the hearts run out, the character dies and needs to start over. The rules of the game are dependent on the conditions met. Without the conditions, there are no rules. With no rules, there is no game.

Connected to this is the motivation behind meeting these certain conditions. No one ever asks other players why they wanted to land on the space that gave them the most money. No one would ever question using the enchanted sword instead of the wooden one. If we are going to play the game, then we are going to follow the conditions to do our best and ultimately succeed. We are not extrinsically motivated to do these things. We are just naturally motivated to do our best while we are in the midst of play.

We firmly believe giving a piece of candy is vastly different than giving out gold for The Game. Although a reluctant student might choose to do an assignment simply to get gold, is the student choosing to do this more as The Game's player or more as a student in an educational system? Most of the time, it is because they want to have a better chance of winning a made-up game where the winners don't even receive a trophy.

Idea #3: In-game motivation can produce intrinsic motivation.

The mission statement of Gamify Education is "Empowering all students to become the best versions of themselves." We use the phrase "best version" a lot with our students. In the early stages of The Game, students could upgrade their original version to their "better version". Of course, this was purposeful.

By the end of playing a classroom game, most students will realize how much stronger their characters have become. At the beginning, they would have gotten trounced by a 1-star monster.

At the end of the year, they would destroy that monster in one turn. The students who transform their characters from super-weak to super-strong will ultimately realize this was not luck. It was through grit and determination, and students will see this in a very tangible way.

At the end of the year, we always ask our hard-working students this question:

"You know, next year you won't have a classroom game to play. What are you going to do then? Are you still going to work hard?"

Time and time again, students answer this the way we would generally expect.

"Now that I know that I can do this, yes, of course, I am going to work hard next year."

Grades. Eligibility. GPA. Scholarships. Admittance into college. If a student needs to transfer some extrinsic motivation of The Game to some other piece of extrinsic motivation, the educational system is not lacking. But for most students, they won't need it. Once they have felt success, there's no going back.

What greater gift could a teacher give to a student than that feeling of success? Afterall, isn't that at the heart and soul of what every teacher wants to instill in their students. What was that called?

That's right.

Intrinsic motivation.

CHAPTER 4:
MORE HESITATIONS

We do have a few more arguments people might make about why gamifying education shouldn't happen. Don't worry, though. These hesitations shouldn't get nearly as deep or as heated as the first one.

Argument #2: By playing a classroom game, you are wasting valuable learning time.

Why on earth would any teacher waste valuable class time making moves on a giant game board and rolling dice to defeat monsters? That can't possibly make any sense, right?

Mr. Lamberson and I share a firm belief that our students need to invest time outside the school day if they want to make a phenomenal amount of growth.

For the first ten years of my teaching career, I had a strict no homework policy (except for independent reading). I remember reading research showing that homework was ineffective at helping students learn. The logic behind it went

like this. **If you send home an assignment to students who already know how to do the skill, you are wasting their time because they aren't learning anything. If you assign homework to students who don't understand the skill, you are wasting your time because the child is going to be completing the work incorrectly and reinforcing the wrong skills. If the child has a parent at home that can help them, neat. But many children in Title I schools don't have that assistance.**

Students who need it don't benefit, and students who don't need it don't benefit. So, I didn't assign homework.

My long-held belief on homework was turned on its head when students got to take devices home. Now, they have a selection of programs to choose from on their computers. Students can use resources like Khan Academy. With these programs, learners are supported when learning new concepts and reinforcing old ones. Feedback is instantaneous. Finally—and this is huge— many of these resources are 100% free.

Because of the 1:1 devices going home, our students now have a chance to be more supported in their learning unlike any other point in history.

But how do you motivate students to *want* to work at home, when there is Snapchat, Facebook, Minecraft, Roblox, Fortnite, Instagram, TikTok, and YouTube? The answer, my dear Watson, is simple.

Motivate them through play.

A lot of our game rewards are based on things they can and should be doing at home. This is one way we justify using precious classroom time to make moves on a map and roll dice to defeat monsters. We believe that our students more than make up for this "loss of instruction time" simply by the extra work they put in outside of the school day. Not every kid will work at home, but we have overwhelming responses on student surveys that say, "I worked harder this year because of The Game."

You need some data to convince you? We got data.

****

If you remember, our school year following the COVID shutdown started with remote learning. Most of the year was followed by hybrid learning. Eventually by the end of the year, we got back all our students in our classrooms at the same time.

That year, the state cancelled its summative test which was normally taken at the end of the year. Why? Because they knew the results would be so dismal that it wouldn't even be worth the time and effort to give the tests. Our district, though, did administer one standardized test called the NWEA Map Test. What is nice about this assessment is there is a report that shows the "Conditional Growth Percentile." This is found by comparing the amount of growth made by the students in a grade level with other students across the nation who started near the same percentiles.

"Well, did gamifying your classrooms improve student learning? Did your students make growth?"

In our district there are seventeen elementary schools. Each elementary school administered the MAP math test, and sixteen out of the seventeen gave the MAP reading test. The school where Mr. Lamberson and I teach is one of the elementary schools listed in the table on the next page.

Here are the results for the Conditional Growth Percentiles of the seventeen elementary schools in our district for the 2020-2021 NWEA Map Tests for math and reading:

	5th Grade Math Conditional Growth Percentile	5th Grade Reading Conditional Growth Percentile
School A	14	2
School B	45	37
School C	43	63
School D	4	29
School E	9	17
School F	14	22
School G	16	2
School H	19	---
School I	45	50
School J	37	63
School K	90	69
School L	12	6
School M	35	4
School N	60	8
School O	22	63
School P	26	6
School Q	98	96

I am sure you can guess which school we are at. But just in case you need the reassurance, yes, Mr. Lamberson and I belong to "School Q".

Not only did our grade level beat all of the other fifth-grade levels in our district pertaining to the Conditional Growth Percentile, we actually beat EVERY elementary grade level in our district. In other words, out of the 85 grade levels in our school district that took the tests, we finished #1.

"Math or reading?"

Both.

****

In case you were looking for some data relating to achievement, we have those results for you, as well.

	5th Grade Math Fall Achievement Percentile	5th Grade Math Spring Achievement Percentile	Percentile Difference from Fall to Spring
School A	3	2	-1
School B	66	64	-2
School C	33	32	-1
School D	47	28	-19
School E	82	69	-13
School F	6	3	-3
School G	19	13	-6
School H	19	14	-5
School I	12	12	0
School J	58	55	-3
School K	65	77	12
School L	68	55	-13
School M	27	24	-3
School N	33	37	4
School O	60	51	-9
School P	14	11	-3
School Q	27	49	22

	5th Grade Reading Achievement Percentile	5th Grade Reading Spring Achievement Percentile	Percentile Difference from Fall to Spring
School A	8	3	-5
School B	83	80	-3
School C	47	51	4
School D	52	46	-6
School E	91	84	-7
School F	20	16	-4
School G	47	26	-21
School H	--	--	--
School I	22	23	1
School J	75	77	2
School K	86	88	2
School L	82	67	-15
School M	64	44	-20
School N	67	51	-16
School O	55	59	4
School P	30	18	-12
School Q	12	27	15

We went from the 10th best school in fifth grade math achievement percentiles to the 7th best. For reading, we went from the 15th best to the 11th best.

Based on the data, the first year we implemented The Game, we...how shall we say this?

We dominated.

Although we are extremely proud of this data, we are equally proud of some other information we collected. At the end of the 2020-2021 year, Mr. Lamberson and I gave our students a short survey. We asked our students if they worked harder because of The Game. 70% of the students said they did indeed work harder because they played a classroom game. 23% chose "neutral". Of these students, many indicated that they would have worked equally as hard with or without a game to play.

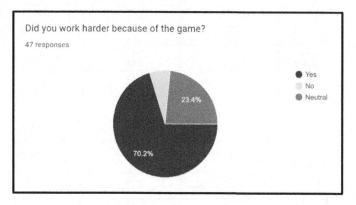

Although I am a math/numbers guy who thoroughly likes coming in first place, maybe my mindset is becoming more of my sister's. Remember how she said that she plays most games for the experience and not necessarily the winning? We also asked our students if they enjoyed playing The Game.

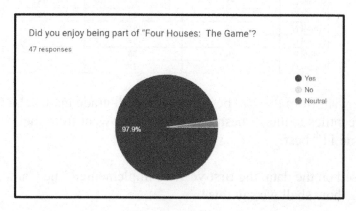

In an era where cyberbullying and suicides are rising at a devastating rate...in an era of brokenness and divisiveness... in an era of teacher burnout depleting its work force...there is great solace knowing that 98% of the students surveyed found enjoyment in something related to school.

That's not saying all of them enjoyed school, but it does show that they enjoyed school *more*.

We know that anecdotal evidence is not as powerful as control groups and sample sizes, but teachers do get empowered from former students coming back and interacting with them. Maybe it's an email. Maybe it's seeing them in Wal-Mart.

I recently was walking down the chip aisle when I saw a former student. Let's call him Jorge.

"Jorge!" I exclaimed as we first made eye contact.

Jorge's first words were not "hello", "Mr. Becker", or "hey". I kid you not, these were the first four words out of his mouth.

"I wanna go back."

I laughed at these first words and asked him why.

"Because of The Game."

It didn't sound like he was doing stellar in school, but he didn't really do stellar for me, either. The Game might not have transformed this apathetic student into an Honor-roll scholar, but for the time I had him in my classroom, I created a learning experience for that student that he thoroughly enjoyed.

Just because there isn't any statistical reliability from Jorge's story, I don't think we should diminish its power.

Time after time, I have the exact same experiences. For the last three years on the first day of school, one former student

always asks me about the changes to this year's classroom game. When I see other former students at the store or picking up their little sisters after school, the interactions all end up the same:

"Are you still playing The Game in your class?"

"Is it the same?"

"Wait, what? You say it's better now? I wish I could play this version."

Then their face drops just a little because they miss having *that* much fun in school.

✱✱✱✱✱✱✱✱✱✱

Let's get back to the argument about how playing a game wastes too much valuable class time.

We are real teachers. We aren't consultants ten years out of the classroom trying to convince you of these things. We have schedules to keep as well as subjects to teach during specific times.

Do you have an extra ten minutes in your schedule that, on paper, says you should be doing one thing but is pretty much a waste? We get it. Use that time. As of writing this book, our students eat breakfast in the classroom. That is when students move on the map and battle it out. Do you know how much "good" learning would take place when students are also eating? Not a lot.

Even if you don't have that spare chunk of ten minutes, you probably have times when you need to give your students a "brain break". There is solid research about giving your students processing time. Use that time. Take five minutes here and five minutes there. Set your own rules and expectations about playing The Game. But we are here to tell you, it doesn't take a lot of actually "playing the game" to make this whole thing successful.

One last note on time. When your students are motivated and engaged, they are working harder. When they are working harder, they get more done. When they get more done, the teacher gets more time.

In a way, *motivational play* creates its own time.

Argument #3: If you create a classroom game, you are just setting your students up for disappointment if their next year's teachers don't have a game.

I hope the people who make this argument never take a family vacation.

All vacations eventually end. Should we never go to the beach or to the mountains because we know that someday we will have to go back home? Should we not do our best to create a fun, enjoyable experience knowing that someday The Game will end?

The comedian, Nate Bargatze, has a great bit about taking his daughter to Disneyland when she was two. A bunch of people told him it was a waste of money because she wouldn't remember anything. His response was to ask those people if he should just lock his daughter in the closet until she got old enough to remember?

"Until you start remembering things, I'm not going to waste any of my money on you, all right?"

Parents take little kids to Disneyland because it makes the kids happy. But parents also do it because it makes them happy to see their kids happy. As a teacher, we hope you find joy watching your students finding joy at school.

Argument #4: Students need to learn the life lesson of plain ol' hard work. Making everything a game is doing a disservice for your students when they get a real job.

There are a lot of college students who work junky jobs to put themselves through college, so they don't have to work those jobs for the rest of their lives. For my mom, it was working at a canning factory. She would sit on a stool for eight hours watching green beans go by on a conveyor belt in a noisy, hot Midwestern factory. If there was a bad bean, she would pick it out.

Eight straight hours of watching green beans.

For me, it was working at a tape factory. My place of employment didn't make the tape, we just sleeved it, boxed it, and shipped it out. Putting tape rolls on a conveyor belt for two straight hours without a break is awfully boring. There are worse jobs, for sure, but waking up at 5:40 AM on a Saturday morning for most college students is not ideal.

All for $7.25 an hour.

I cleaned carpet, worked as a janitor at an auto body shop— yes, it was disgusting cleaning up after 30 guys—where I was also a night shift tow truck driver, and taught violin/guitar lessons while getting my teaching degree. All at the same time. There are no smells or sounds that affect me. I am immune. In a way, it was brilliant training for becoming a teacher.

On the weekends at the tape factory, the only crew that worked was the College Crew. Our supervisors were schoolmates and often our friends. As the adage goes, "When the boss is away, the workers will play."

We created a game. It was a real-life baseball game in the middle of this tape factory. We rolled up a bunch of plastic wrap and taped it into a ball. We found an old 2x4 and used it as a bat. We pitched. We batted. We hit home runs over the machines. It was epic.

"Wouldn't your real boss figure out that you stopped work early to play a game? Wouldn't your quota numbers suffer?"

In that small tape factory in the middle of Minnesota lies a philosophy about human effort and rewards. We never lied on our quota numbers. We wrote down what we accomplished. We just outperformed the non-College Crew in seven hours of work than they did in eight. We would discuss it at break, "If we work really hard for the next couple hours, we can play 'tapeball' at the end of the day."

We worked hard, got our numbers to look good, and took the extra time off to hit around a plastic ball of shrink wrap with an old piece of wood.

Say what you will about our ethics, but we made that company more money while playing a baseball game than the normal crew did while not playing a game.

"Why didn't you try just as hard for the full eight hours of work?"

In a perfect world, we would have. We just weren't motivated. Neither was the non-College Crew. Throughout the week, we worked alongside this other crew. During a break in the lunchroom one night, I remember having a conversation about this exact thing. My friends and I were switched to a different job because we were faster and had a higher percentage of standard met. I tried telling this worker from the other crew how we were able to achieve such a high standard by doing something different.

She couldn't have been more disinterested. She wouldn't even let me tell her how to improve efficiency. When I was about to, she literally stopped me midsentence and said, "They don't pay me enough to do that."

For my first job. I was basically running a lawn mowing operation for a company called Mow Money.

Mow Money?

Seriously, it was called Mow Money. One day I went to my boss and said, "Hey, if we rearrange the route, we can get the lawns done faster." I got permission and turned a normal eight-hour day into a four-hour day by switching up the routes.

Just so you know, Mr. Lamberson was an hourly worker. If you are following the story, you are correct. Mr. Lamberson voluntarily cut his own hours, effectively making himself poorer.

I wasn't working for the money. I was working for the summer between my first and second year in college. I didn't actually want a job, but my parents wanted me to have one if I was going to live at home. Since I wasn't too keen on the idea of paying rent for an apartment, I took this job. The faster I got done, the sooner I could go hangout with my future wife and enjoy the gorgeous summer days.

We're going to let you draw your own conclusions from these studies of human psychology, but we will make one point. If you can convince students that play and hard work can exist together, maybe you are shaping students to be drawn to future jobs where this can occur. Maybe they will seek out a job where they are free to be creative, autonomous, and more in control of when and how a task needs to be done. And who knows? Maybe they will find so much fun in the work itself that they will stop playing "tapeball" during their last hour on the clock.

Argument #5: In my classroom, a game isn't really needed.

You might not like this, reader, but we are going to concede this argument. You really might be a teacher who doesn't need a game. If you are nodding your head right now, I am guessing you don't have very many apathetic students.

Don't get too offended, but I don't think teaching in your classroom would be that difficult.

For example, if you are teaching a senior honors ELA class, a game could be more of a distraction than what it's worth. The students know that if they don't do their work, they won't pass the AP test and get college credit.

I took AP Lit and only read half a book all year. I wrote all my essays for the test based on that one book, *One Who Flew Over the Cuckoo's Nest*. I passed. Not all AP kids are motivated; some are just cocky.

If you are teaching a middle school elective in which students get to make movies and do photography, I doubt you need a game to motivate these kids who picked your elective class.

Great. You don't need a game. You're not worried about those students. I'm not worried about those students.

I'm concerned about the ones who aren't motivated—the kids who don't have the opportunity to pick fun elective classes because they are now stuck with double ELA and double math blocks. These are the kids who need a game. These are the kids who need you to set one up.

But again, even the motivated kids would still have an epic time. Have you already forgotten?

Where's the fun?

CHAPTER 5:
THE GAME

You might think I am not a nice person because I have made you wait this long to actually talk about The Game. You might be additionally frustrated that I have annoyingly referred to The Game with a capital T and a capital G. I should tell you there's a good reason for it. It's because you couldn't handle The Game.

You want THE GAME? You can't handle THE GAME!... sorry.

Maybe you could. There's probably a handful of teachers in each district that could. Most teachers couldn't. Even more wouldn't want to. Unless you have a collection of complex board games on your shelves at home, I don't think The Game would have fit your needs as a teacher.

That's why I have been making you wait this long. I wanted to get you hooked on this wonderful, chaotic idea of transforming your classroom into a game without even telling you what type of game we played. But that time is over.

Hmmm...I don't even know where to begin.

<deep breath>

Alright. I got this. Here we go:

The Game was an RPG-styled game in which each student got to choose one of six characters: a hunter, a mage, a healer, a knight, a swordsman/swordswoman, or a warrior. Each type of hero had a unique avatar, but it could change depending on which element the student chose: water, fire, earth, or wind. Each student's character got different stats based on which hero they chose. The stats were in the following categories: health points (HP), attack, skill, dodge, defense, and resistance. Students could acquire equipment that would boost their stats. There were different monsters the students could battle. They could even battle each other. I initially had an Excel spreadsheet that was our Battle Simulator. Since then, we transitioned to rolling six-sided dice and eight-sided dice. Students could play different cards to alter their stats. When they reached Level 30, they could spend their gold to get promoted to a stronger character with a new avatar. Oh, and there was a map! A giant map where 65 players from three fifth grade classes all moved around. The winner of the original game was whoever could defeat the final boss.

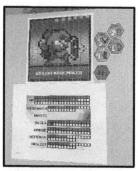

Figure 1: One of the first characters ever created with its stat sheet. The pixel art sure has improved with time.

Phew. Made it.

Nice, but even that was like the 30,000-foot view. To really explain the whole game, it would literally take a book of its own.

Figure 2: Our original map in which students tried to control territories.

As far as we knew, no one had done what we were doing at the same level. With no one to copy, we kept trying ideas which led to new ones. Equipment was created. Cards were made to negate the equipment. Other cards were created to negate the negation. This eventually led to the previous rambling paragraph in which most of the teacher population lost interest after the acronym, RPG.

Figure 3: The map at the end of the second year playing The Game.

Your Game doesn't need to be The Game. And it shouldn't be. Our game was way too complicated.

Mr. Lamberson and I are confident that we can help all teachers transform their classrooms into a giant game. I have read a lot of the books out there on gamifying education. Mr. Lamberson and I even attended a virtual PD about gamifying education that our state Department of Education hosted. Although there are numerous resources available to teachers about gamifying their classrooms, we feel there is just as much *unhelpful* information out there as there is helpful information.

Figure 4: The Game got complex early on with the addition of cards.

Before we talk about the unhelpful recommendations, we want to preface this by saying that some of these original resources provided great inspiration to get us on the path we are currently on. If it wasn't for that article about a teacher out East in February of 2021, you more than likely would not be reading this book.

For that, we do thank you, whoever you are, and for all those trying to help motivate students in our current culture.

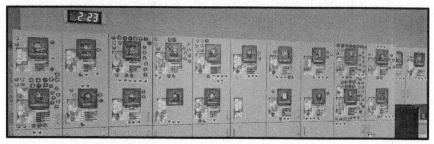

Figure 5: How sweet it looks! This is what my classroom looked like at the end of the 22-23 school year.

Now that we acknowledged that, the biggest frustration Mr. Lamberson and I have with the resources out there is the following elevator pitch sent to teachers:

"Gamify your classroom and watch your students become engaged like they have never been before! As the teacher, pick a classroom theme. If you like outer space, use planets, stars, and spacecrafts. If you like sports, use players and coaches as characters in your game. If you teach about Westward Expansion, then maybe you want a Wild West theme. You can do whatever you want!

Use a leaderboard to track the progress of your students. The higher they go on the leaderboard, the more powerful equipment they can earn. Experience points can help show the more dominant players in the game. Gold can be used to buy additional equipment.

Students will thoroughly enjoy being transformed into a different reality. They will be having so much fun, they will forget they are actually learning. Any questions?"

Yes, I have a question.

How?

That is the question that you will be hard pressed to find the answer to in so many of the resources out there on gamifying education. And yet, that is the *most* important question for any teacher.

Have you ever been to the Cheesecake Factory? No, it's not just a bakery where they serve cheesecake. It's a full-fledged restaurant with a really confusing name. Do you know how many menu items the Cheesecake Factory has? 250.

Let that sink in. The most time-consuming part of eating at the Cheesecake Factory is deciding what you are going to eat. I will pour over the menu multiple times until I undoubtedly land on eating the same thing every time. Why? It's a psychological effect called choice paralysis. When given too many choices our brains have a difficult time making decisions as to what we want.

We aren't going to give you 1001 ways you can gamify your classroom. In fact, you are going to be surprised just how low the number actually is.

You might be feeling a little nervous right now, wondering how you can take a limitless idea and fit it within the four walls of your classroom. We got you.

Mr. Lamberson and I have narrowed down this overwhelming, chaotic, magical idea of creating a classroom game into four basic principles which we have eloquently named, THE FOUR CORNERSTONES OF GAMIFY EDUCATION.

I hope you read that in a booming, echoing voice.

We are convinced that if you implement these four basic principles, you will find success utilizing a game to increase student motivation and joy.

Get ready then, for the First Cornerstone of Gamify Education.

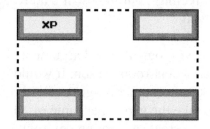

CHAPTER 6:
EXPERIENCE POINTS

I have zero clue who was the first one in the game business to coin the phrase "XP". I do know that thousands of games now use this mechanic.

For me, it was Finally Fantasy VII on the original PlayStation.

XP (can you see why it stands for "EX-perience P-oints?) is a simple, yet ingenious way to get players more invested in a game. Regardless of the type of game, it's always the same: getting better, stronger, wiser, or more accurate is quantified with a number. As a logical thinker who loves order, this makes me feel good. I know exactly how many more points I need before my character gets "leveled up", meaning they are going to get some reward for being better. This could be a better chance to make a three pointer or more strength to defeat a monster.

There's something intrinsically human about the good feelings players get when they take a guy who can barely catch a football to him winning the National Championship. Or when they change a low-level mutant who can barely lift a garbage can to one that can destroy a robot with her brain.

I don't even know if game designers can pinpoint the power behind these good feelings, but I know it's there. And it's there in your students, as well.

However, a platform of logical coded arguments in a video game is much different than a classroom lesson. It would be impossible to run a classroom like a computer program. But I don't think that is a bad thing. We can take the game mechanic of XP, combined with the art of teaching, to create a learning environment in which students get these same strong feelings of accomplishment.

Dopamine is the chemical that is released in your brain which makes you repeat behaviors and form habits. That's literally its purpose. If you are out in the forest and you find a delicious berry, your brain releases dopamine making the experience pleasurable. Then, your brain seeks to have that experience again, so you seek the same berries out. After a while, the berries become part of your diet and are a habit.

One way to produce these strong feelings of accomplishment in your students is by handing out XP chips. Our first installment of XP was wooden hexes. I was initially thinking about a tabletop game I could create using hexagons, so I bought hundreds of them off Amazon. But after a year of trying to develop the tabletop game, I gave up.

Yes, my wife was also wondering why I had spent so much money on hexes before I actually had the game's idea more established. But never fear, my wife, I found a use for them.

But there was a glaring problem. The hexes were blank. Mr. Lamberson found the solution, **"Why don't you make a stamp and stamp them all?"**

Do you know what never followed?

"Let me help you stamp all the hexes."

Doesn't the Oracle just sit around her apartment all day yelling at kids not to pick their noses?

I'd like to point out that you never asked for help. I believe you completed this task at home. Also, yes, I'm more of an ideas man.

The hexes worked, but we're not suggesting those to you. Pull out the bag of tangrams from your cupboard that seven teachers ago stuffed in there and assign values to the different shapes. Go to Home Depot, get a dowel, and cut it into pucks.

Figure 6: Some of the wooden hexes Mr. Lamberson never helped stamp.

The XP chips really just need values assigned to them. They don't even need numbers. Different colors are probably even more important. That was the problem with the hexes. They all looked the same. Too often, I would find myself shuffling through all these different tokens looking for a 50, but all I could ever find were 5's and 15's.

That's why I switched to poker chips. Different colored poker chips with different numbers on them—the best of both worlds. I bought a bunch of them off Amazon because I didn't want to go to rummage sales looking for Grandma's sets she no longer wants. The poker chips

Figure 7: I got really annoyed that the stamps weren't perfect.

I bought had values of 5's, 10's, 25's, 50's, and 100's. These denominations work well for student XP.

I will tell you that there is no greater sound and no greater smile on the face of a student when they dump out their pouch of poker chips, waiting for you to count them all. I like to put on a front and say, "What do you mean? I have to count all of these?"

The smile gets even bigger then.

If you live in a state or work in a district that has some connotations with poker chips and gambling, then type, "Blank plastic circles" into Amazon. I have no doubt you can get creative.

Figure 8: The poker chips I use for XP.

Mr. Lamberson and I each teach our group of kids for most of the day. They have a desk and have no problem collecting their XP chips in little pouches we give them. If you are a middle or high school teacher, then maybe physical XP tokens is not the way to go. Maybe you need something digital.

I still use the wooden hexagons because I like the feel of them. It really and truly doesn't matter what you use for your XP, but what does matter—especially at the elementary level—is that you are handing them a physical item when they learn. This is important. It needs to be something the student can touch and see as a constant reminder of their success. There is something satisfying about children having fat stacks of XP on their desks for all their peers to admire. Digital would be a last resort.

Okay. You have your XP tokens, or at least you can picture them in your mind. Now what? What happens with the XP tokens in the hands of the teacher? It's quite simple: XP is given for student learning.

XP is not for student effort. It needs to be a student's proof of learning something. When students show they have learned, then they earn XP.

The freedom this gives teachers is why XP is the First Cornerstone of Gamify Education. Here's the power of your cheap piece of plastic or wooden hex called an XP chip. You are the teacher. You get to decide what is worthy of earning XP and what is not. You have chapter math tests? Great. Hand out a bunch of XP for those. You expect your students to write a five-page paper? Woah. That better be a lot of XP. You got an exit ticket for addition? Great. Give them 10 XP if they get it right on their first try. You will try something, and it might not work out the best. Big deal. Be the Oracle. Or the Architect. I still don't quite understand Mr. Lamberson's *Matrix* references.

Later, we will give you more guidance about just how much XP you should give out over the course of the year. For now, just remember XP is for learning.

Remember Mr. Becker and his Spanish streak? One day, interrupting his Spanish lesson as he finished his lunch, I asked him, "What if we build streaks into the game?"

Mr. Becker was intrigued.

I went on to explain my idea. For completing a reading log every week, students would be able to build a streak. When they would reach a certain number, they would get extra moves on the map in our game.

We tried it.

The results were mixed. Most students really didn't care about the streak. They may have gotten one or two weeks, but then they lost it and quit trying altogether. They felt defeated having lost their streak and all the extra moves they had earned.

We found that once students lost their streaks, their effort toward reading at home was typically worse than it was before the streak bonus was implemented.

What was the lesson we learned? Not all gaming elements work in the classroom. Some need tweaking. If we were to do streaks again, we wouldn't take students back to the start. We would just remove one week. This way, student effort wouldn't be completely decimated.

Do we regret this experiment? Heck no! You will never find the secret sauce unless you try different ingredients.

We are definitely not the first—or the last—to tout the handing out of XP in a classroom. There are some even really fancy online games where students go on missions and level up characters that way. Their characters were designed by graphic artists and the students get to play an actual video game in which they earn XP.

Although those options look promising, I don't think they can fulfill what a classroom teacher needs. Mr. Lamberson and I have 78 math learning targets to teach. Are there 78 specific missions in that video game that correspond to each of our learning targets?

No. There's like four.

We also focus on the formation of the United States of America. Does the online video game have specific missions about the Stamp Act and the Sons of Liberty?

No, again.

That's a real problem. We admit that on some days, for some lessons, there are cooler things out there. But unless that cool thing can be embedded throughout your entire year's material, you are going to piece a bunch of different things together. That might work for a few of you, but that wouldn't work for me and most of the teacher population.

With XP as a foundational component of The Game, teachers can merge the entire curriculum with play.

Using *motivational play* is a way to make learning the thing that

58

students desire. We have found that students at first want to learn to get better in The Game, but once they have a taste of success from their learning, they want to learn to show they are better in The Game. This distinction is very important.

Give me a second to wrap my head around that slice of advice.

Time and time again, students keep working hard because they want to see how high they can fly. Even when the incentives become more infrequent, the students who truly take off never come back down.

"I get it so far, but what is all this XP for?"

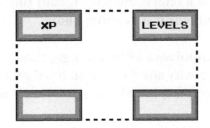

CHAPTER 7:
LEVELS

Level 1 is super weak. Level 45 is tremendous. Level 70 is unheard of. A lot of video games that use XP also use levels. It's a combination of game mechanics that is tried and true. There are lots of ways to assign levels to your students with the use of XP. However, we strongly encourage you to copy how we level up our students.

Every student starts at Level 1. In order to advance out of Level 1, a student needs 10 XP. To get out of Level 2 and advance to Level 3, a student needs 20 XP. Simply put, to advance out of the current level, it takes 10x the experience points. To advance out of Level 70, it would take 700 XP. No one can possibly get to Level 70, right?

False.

We've got to talk about a student of mine during the second year of playing The Game. Let's call her Dream. Our district gives an intelligence screening assessment to 2nd graders to see if they qualify for the Gifted and Talented Special Programs. Dream qualified for this. She was undoubtedly gifted. Her

parents were refugees who believed in the power of hard work. They also seemed to believe in the dangers of too much technology. For that apparent reason, Dream did not have a cell phone or even a television. This meant that her only real form of entertainment was reading books.

Dream had an abundance of two things: time and boredom. When I asked her why she worked so hard at home, she told me, "Mr. Lamberson, I can either read, do Khan Academy, or do chores."

Dream's sister had come through our school just the year before and was a tremendous student herself. Both Dream and her sister were amazing readers and eager learners.

Alright, reader, this is as close as we are going to get to a "control group".

Dream loved The Game, which hopefully answers the question you may be thinking. Yes, girls love playing a classroom game just as much as the boys do—maybe even more.

At first, Dream's character became extremely powerful just because her normal efforts were so much greater than the average student's. But she never showcased her strength. One day, I encouraged her to go fight a monster on the map, promising her that she would do well in the battle.

Remember how we said earlier that The Game cannot be based on luck? This is why.

Dream crushed the monster with prejudice. From that moment on, she was all in. She wanted to conquer every monster on the map. By the end of the year, she was one of two students who defeated The Game's final boss.

What may be most interesting is the fact that Dream's character reached maximum stats in February of that school year. Did Dream stop working hard? No, she wanted to see

how high she could climb. By the end of the year, Dream had reached Level 76.

Now, if you remember the rule for advancing out of the level, it is always 10x more than the level itself. So, when Dream went from Level 75 to Level 76, she needed to earn 750 XP. Do you wonder about just how much XP she earned throughout the course of the year? Well...

$$750 + 740 + 730 + 720 + 710 + 700 + 690 + ... + 20 + 10 = 28,500 \text{ XP}$$

That is absurd.

We kept track of these levels by printing out hexagons with different numbers on them. We used a colored printer, cardstock, and a hexagon hole punch. We then attached the scratchy side of Velcro® to the hex and the soft side on the classroom's cabinet. When I was making all these level hexes, I stopped at Level 60, thinking to myself, "There is no way any child is going to ever get this high."

Figure 9: The hexagon-shaped levels that didn't go past Level 60.

I even underestimated the power of a classroom game.

In the previous year, Dream finished near the 85th percentile for both reading and math. At the end of fifth grade, she was above the 95th for both. She went from great to exceptional.

Maybe we shouldn't compare siblings, but for the sake of our one control group with a sample size of one, I feel like we must. Dream outperformed her older sister...and it wasn't even that close.

✳✳✳✳✳✳✳✳✳✳

What about those students who don't come in already killing it? Let me tell you about Lily.

After the first full year of playing The Game, we decided to create a Hall of Fame. Each teacher got to choose one or more students who deserved special recognition for their exceptional fifth-grade exploits. I chose Dream.

Figure 10: We stuck the level next to the student's character on the cabinets.

If a student makes it to the Hall of Fame, that student gets a framed picture that is literally hanging in the hall of our school. The picture includes the character's avatar, the student's name, the character's name, and the level of the character.

Lily was a quiet, former homeschooler who came to my classroom as her first public school experience. She would walk under Dream's framed Hall of Fame photo every morning.

I would tell the kids of Dream's achievements and how I believed her accomplishments were the highest level of achievement a student could reach.

Lily sat back and thought, "Hold my beverage."

Using roughly the same system of handing out XP, Lily did what I thought would be impossible. She reached Level 123. Unlike Dream, Lily was not a "gifted child" as the district would define her. But she definitely was. In her quest to be the best in The Game, her true capabilities were revealed.

✶✶✶✶✶✶✶✶✶✶

Hopefully, you are still following us. Teachers give out XP to students who show learning. Students collect these XP chips. At some point then, they need to turn these XP chips back into the teacher for a level upgrade. We call this "Leveling Up."

Leveling Up is the chance for the teacher to conference with each individual student for 3-5 minutes once per week. When called, the student brings back any XP she has earned. She also brings back her reading log for the week and is ready to tell the teacher if she made any "milestones" in Khan Academy or Accelerated Reader.

Milestones are certain thresholds that, when met, rain down game rewards. You can create milestone rewards for students reading books, learning their math facts, or doing a class presentation. It's up to you.

At this point, the teacher checks in on their progress and gives feedback and encouragement. More importantly to The Game, though, this is when the teacher counts up all of the XP and changes the character's level if enough XP was earned.

We keep track of this on a Google Sheet. I even came up with some formulas in which the calculations are done automatically, so I don't have to sit there figuring out the math. (If you bought a non-audio version of this book, a template with these formulas can be found in the appendix.)

FIRE GUILD					
	Starting Level	Starting XP	Earned XP	New Level	New XP	GOLD
xxxx	1	0	0	1	0	
xxxx	1	0	0	1	0	
xxxx	1	0	0	1	0	
xxxx	1	0	0	1	0	
xxxx	1	0	0	1	0	
xxxx	1	0	0	1	0	
xxxx	1	0	0	1	0	
xxxx	1	0	0	1	0	

Figure 11. This is how we keep track of the XP and Levels in Google Sheets.

Since this can get a bit complicated, let me give you an example showing how XP is traded in for a Level upgrade:

Kiesha, starting the year at Level 1 and 0 XP, earned 40 XP the first week of school. Since it takes 10 XP to get out of Level 1, 20 XP to get out of Level 2, and 30 XP to get out of Level 3, Kiesha has enough XP to get out of Level 1 and Level 2, but not quite enough to get out of Level 3. So, for now, Kiesha's character is a Level 3. But, it's not a Level 3 with 0 XP. She still has 10 XP leftover. You could give a 10 XP chip back to Kiesha, or you can keep it in the "bank" for her.

If you are using a Google Sheet like ours, her new "Starting Level" would be 3 with 10 for her "Starting XP".

The next week Kiesha earned 60 XP. With her 10 XP leftover from before, she really has 70 XP to get out of Level 3. Since it takes 30 XP to get out of Level 3 and 40 XP to get out of Level 4, Kiesha has advanced to Level 5 (with 0 XP leftover).

If you are using the Google Sheet, just type 60 into the "Earned XP" with a "Starting Level" of 3 and "Starting XP" of 10. If your formulas are correct, the "New Level" should say 5 and the "New XP" should say 0.

✱✱✱✱✱✱✱✱✱✱

A student's level should be a direct picture of how much success that student has found at that given point in time.

A few days before the first day of school, families come into the school to meet the teachers, see the classrooms, and get a broad overview of what the school year will hold. I don't talk much about The Game, but with the pictures on the cabinets and the giant avatars above the windows, it naturally comes up. A father once asked me about the pictures on the cabinets, specifically pointing to the one with his son's name on it.

"So, you're telling me that all students start at Level 1, and they gain levels by doing their work?"

"Yup."

"That's smart. It must be a good way to keep track of how well they are doing."

"That's the goal."

"I wish I had that when I went to school. I was never good at school. The truth is I didn't know how to read, even when I was in high school. I caused a lot of trouble, so the school just kept passing me along."

That turned heavy. I never met this man before in my life, and he opened a window to his own educational experience by looking at his child's avatar on my classroom cabinet. He understood what the levels meant, and it wasn't how powerful the character would be in The Game. It was a direct reflection on how well the student was doing academically at that given moment.

I wonder if he brought up his own educational experiences because he thought he might have been a low-level character the entire year. You might be asking what to do with students like that.

I was scrolling through my old text messages the other day, and my brother asked a very similar question, "What happens if a kid doesn't get any power-ups and is behind the entire year?"

The answer can be found embedded in the Third Cornerstone of Gamify Education: Differentiation.

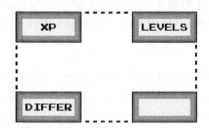

CHAPTER 8:
DIFFERENTIATION

When I was going through college, there was an old saying that kept getting repeated:

"Don't be the sage on the stage; be the guide on the side."

While the sentiment was good, it had some unintended consequences. What was being said was, "Be there and work with each student individually to meet their needs while they discover learning for themselves." What was heard was, "Let the kids figure it out on their own."

My father-in-law, when he worked as a middle school gym teacher, would often ask the kids, "How was the packet today in so-and-so's class?"

"How'd you know we did a packet?" the kids would say as they cocked back their heads.

"Just a hunch," he responded with a smile.

He called them packet assembly lines. The teacher in question would have neat stacks of papers set out for the students as they walked into the classroom. They would go down the line collecting pages and then staple them all together. The remainder of the period was spent working on the packet. The goal being the completion of the packet, not the learning of content.

For my whole career up until this point, I had been a "direct instruction" guy. Not a didactic sage on the stage, but a Socratic conversationalist. I value classroom conversations and the awe of group discovery. But there are also times when students need to step up and perform on their own.

The Greeks had a philosophy called the golden mean. Basically, the idea is that in all things, the answer is usually in the middle. The story of Daedalus and Icarus has a theme reflecting this philosophy. Don't fly too close to the water; don't fly too close to the sun. Stay in the middle.

I believe this philosophy has a lot of truth in the world and in education. What's the best approach for instructing students? I believe it is the balanced approach: one where students learn through conversation but where they are also accountable for their own learning.

What does this all have to do with differentiation?

Let's go back to the packet teachers. If everyone is getting the same packet regardless of reading ability, background knowledge, critical thinking skills, etc., then the work is far too easy for some students and far too difficult for others. It's not tailored learning. For students to be learning the maximum amount of information, they need to be in their zone of proximal development.

The ZPD. I always felt that more acronyms should use a "z".

We now live in an era where learning can be tailored to each individual student, so that most of the time, they are working

in their ZPD. This is critical to a high-functioning classroom.

We *can* be the guide on the side. In our current age of technology, it is easier than ever. Using *motivation play* in your classroom gives you a vehicle to drive differentiation. But it's not just a nice thing you can do in your room, it is essential for this work.

Becker, go.

My younger brother was a classroom teacher at a choice school in inner-city Milwaukee for multiple years before he moved to the administration side of things where he currently resides. When I first started pitching the idea of gamifying education to him, he told me something incredibly important:

"Just make sure the smartest students aren't only the most powerful characters in the game."

Most teachers would say "obviously" or something like that. But if I pressed you a little harder on how you would make sure this quotation proved true, you might hesitate for a bit. Implementing this is hard—really hard. Mr. Lamberson and I discussed this idea for a long time, over the course of 1.5 school years.

Nowadays, this is what we invest most of our efforts into. We spend very little time on the actual mechanics of The Game. Most of our thought and work goes into creating equitable outcomes.

Nearly every other day, our students take a math quiz. It's a relatively-short, 8-point quiz based on a specific fifth-grade math standard. We're going to pose a question to you, and then we want you to pause and think about what you would do. Please don't go reading ahead without first reflecting on what you would do as a teacher. Here's the question:

"In a fifth-grade math classroom made up of students spanning the 1st percentile to the 90th percentile, how would you distribute XP so that the XP is differentiated and equitable?"

<pause>

Mr. Lamberson and I argued whether all our students should be expected to take quizzes on the fifth-grade learning targets and not fourth or third-grade level targets. We talked about whether some of the fifth-grade quizzes should be easier and some of the quizzes be more difficult. We discussed what we should do with the students who were at the first percentile. We tried to figure out if we would give more XP to the students who started lower and less XP to the students who started higher. Or, we thought, should we give the same XP to all students, but differ the number of points needed to gain the XP?

Complicated, right? Welcome to one of the weakest aspects of our current educational system.

Tell me if this is familiar. Have you ever heard of a reading incentive program that gave out rewards to the kid who read the most books or earned the most points? Did those kids get a longer recess, a better prize, or even the chance to win a new bike?

What about the kids who were in the same grade but were significantly lower in reading? Did the low-level readers ever stand a chance against the high readers in the grade?

I doubt it.

Most of the time the rewards go to the student who can learn the most or be the best. Sometimes, though, the low-performing students are the ones being targeted:

"Jimmy, you've been in the red zone the entire week. If you can somehow make it to the orange zone today, then I'm going to give you a pencil."

In both scenarios, do you know who is consistently forgotten?

The average kid.

Yes, the type of kid who makes up the majority of the classroom is forgotten because he is neither "that good" or "that bad".

What's more impressive? A kid who comes in at the 87th percentile in a given area and gets to the 93rd percentile, or a kid who comes in at the 15th percentile and gets to the 40th? In my opinion, they are equally impressive and deserve equal reward.

As a teacher, then, you need to make conscious decisions about differentiating the amount of XP given so that the high kids aren't only the strongest characters, so the average kids have a true chance to become dominant, and so the low-performing students start viewing themselves as highly capable.

We already told you that this is not easy.

Whether you like it or not, you must use some sort of ability grouping. I guess there is a good reason for all those standardized tests our students are forced to take. Based on the data, Mr. Lamberson and I split our students into three or four groups for math and ELA. Once the reward tiers are set, students stay in that "tier" for the rest of the year.

That's really important. Don't "punish" a student who never operated at the 70th percentile a lower amount of XP because he finally reached that level. Keep rewarding that student with the same amount of XP he earned at the beginning of the year. If you move that kid up, he will rarely catch up to the student who started much higher than him, thus violating this very important cornerstone.

Are you beginning to think about how you can differentiate your rewards? Just to be sure, here's a list of things you can never say:

"I'm going to give 100 XP for A's, 75 XP for B's, ..."

"If everyone on your team gets above an 80%, then..."

"Whoever does the best on this quiz will get a game bonus."

"[To everybody] Once you hit 10 points, you get..."

****

It was my junior year of high school. Instead of a final exam, my ELA teacher gave this huge assignment that would count as 20% of our semester grade. The project involved finding examples from different works of classic literature. The teacher said that the student who came up with the most accurate examples would set the curve.

After hours of hard work, I was confident that my 80-something examples would get me close to the A. Well, my over-achieving-soon-to-be-accepted-into-Westpoint friend decided to submit a terrifying 160 examples. My clear evidence of meeting the standard with 80 examples earned me a solid B-. That single project ruined my 4.0.

I graduated high school twenty years ago. I still feel that it was unfair.

How do you think that low-level reader feels when he is constantly compared to that high-level reader when the reading rewards are given out?

It really is inequitable when we do things like this. You need to protect your students when building Your Game—or any system, really—on this cornerstone.

It's not easy, but it is probably the most important thing you can do for your students if you want to build confidence, self-esteem, and an overall sense of pride.

Don't do the work, and twenty years later a disgruntled, former student might write about you in a book he wrote.

****

How are you going to differentiate the XP given out in your classroom?

For math, Mr. Lamberson and I decided that we would not drop the academic bar for our 8-point quizzes, meaning every student would take the same quiz and need to score a 6 or higher. For the students in the upper tier, we would give them 15 XP. For the students in the middle tier, we would give them 40 XP. For the ones in the lowest tier, we would give them 100 XP if they could pass the quiz with a 6 or higher.

Was it the only way to differentiate the reward for learning? Of course not. Honestly, it wasn't even the best way. For ELA, we decided on something different.

Every week, our students took a relatively short, 8-question quiz on the reading selection of the week. Every student had a chance to earn 50 XP. For the high-level readers, they needed a 7 or 8. The middle level readers needed a 6 or higher; the low-level readers needed to get at least 5 correct. For the students brand new to the country who knew very little English, they could earn their 50 XP by getting a 3 or better.

As we reflect on what was the most equitable, it's more of what we did for ELA and not as much for math. Regardless of which method you choose, though, you are still miles ahead of thinking about equitable differentiation compared to the general, sorry state of education.

Something my father-in-law taught me was that a good teacher

is like a really good coach. He would know. He had one of the best coaches on the planet at his time wrestling Division I at Arizona State University. For the wrestling fans out there, the coach was Bobby Douglas.

Good coaches study each individual athlete to diagnose weaknesses. They then set a program for individual skills and conditioning. They push the athlete to follow the prescription. The coaches then evaluate if the programming was successful or not, and then they make a new prescription based on the athlete's needs.

The National Board's "Architecture of Accomplished Teaching" has an incredibly similar model.

Turning 30 was a hard pill for me to swallow. I became determined to get strong. I set a goal to lift 405 pounds on my back squat. The first-time squatting, did I throw 405 pounds on the bar? Obviously not. That could have killed me.

Literally.

I started at the weight I could handle and put in the work building strength. Over the course of three years, I was able to put in enough work and gain enough weight to be able to achieve my goal.

Learning is the same. If you hand a fifth-grade text to a student who is brand new to the English language and say, "Go read this," you are metaphorically sticking 405 pounds on his back. All you will do is crush him. It is imperative that you find the correct "weight" for each student to make the maximum gain. It needs to be doable, but also an uncomfortable struggle.

That's hitting their ZPD.

Let's make this perfectly clear. The differentiation of XP earned is not about equality of outcomes for all individuals regardless of the work or effort. It is about honoring the work and effort of all students at their ability levels and the relative effort they had to exert to reach that level. If two students both achieve success at their relative abilities, they are equally successful.

This does not mean that you pass students who don't work hard. You will still have students who fail. Differentiation is about honoring relative effort and relative learning achievement, not laziness.

When we first started implementing "milestones" for Khan Academy, the students who were on level had no problem seeing the toil as worthwhile to gain their XP bonuses. But for the lower-level kids, it was too much. Years later, we created a system where the lower-level students could get XP for each practice. This meant they would get handed small chunks of XP throughout the day, every day, over the course of a week and month. This motivated these students to continue to work. This was a game changer for so many of the kids who, historically, were on the bottom rung of learning achievement.

Even this is differentiation.

✶✶✶✶✶✶✶✶✶✶

You have had ample time to think about what my brother asked, "What happens if kids don't get any power-ups and are behind the entire year?"

What would your answer be to him? Is it okay for students to be Level 14, super-weak characters in June?

Mr. Lamberson and I share some similar personality traits. One of these traits is that we are not very sympathetic people. It is easy for us to say, "Of course it's okay for students to be Level 14, super-weak characters at the end of the year!"

77

But it really has nothing to do with us being unsympathetic.

There are some serious issues with the public educational system in the United States of America. One of the biggest issues we have is the fake, you-don't-get-what-you-earned fantasy world that we have created for many elementary and middle-school students. I am reminded of this almost every day in which I teach math. It's such a struggle because I need to teach third-grade math, fourth-grade math, and fifth-grade math in my one block. I don't want to sound whiny, but…

"What is area?" I ask.

"I don't know," multiple students say.

"Adding up the sides," is the answer from a different student.

"No."

"Multiplying the length and width," comes from a generally-high student.

"No. That's not what area *is*."

"That's what my teacher taught me."

"We got a lot of work to do."

First of all, how do so many of my fifth-grade students not know what area is by the time they reach me? There are seven distinct standards that relate to area in third grade. But year after year, many students do not have the proper understanding of this mathematical concept.

Why?—and don't say "COVID".

Many students are going to advance to fourth grade whether they master third-grade math or not. Those students could continue to advance without ever actually understanding their grade-level math. Far too often, we have created a fantasy world for too many students in too many districts in too many states.

(Disclaimer: I am not talking about all students. I am also not referring to students who have learning disabilities. These students have had disabilities identified and require special services to help meet their individual needs. The vast majority of students who get passed along without meeting standards do not have a disability. Also, some of my students who have shown the most growth over the course of my fifteen-year career also had IEPs.)

Simply put, students have gained their rewards with very little effort.

Middle schools might operate the same way, but most high schools do not. In high school, an F carries weight. Lack of credit. Loss of extracurricular activities. No diploma. These are real consequences. The make-believe world has shattered. "Real life" begins.

What on earth are we doing then? We are teaching—yes, teaching!—that apathy yields no negative consequences. Until they do. And when that happens, it is sadly too late for some to ever be caught up.

So, is it okay for a student to stare at his low level on the cabinet wall all year long?

Absolutely.

Here you might disagree with us. You wouldn't be the first or the last. Some opponents to this philosophy have accused us of "shaming" students.

The s-word.

During the COVID shutdown, I did a lot of professional development. I "attended" a virtual seminar about school leadership and social-emotional learning. I wish I could remember who I was listening to, but the expert speaker said there is a difference between guilt and shame.

Truer words have never been spoken.

How can we be shaming students when they all start at the same level? How can we shame students when we have tiered the XP so even the lowest-achieving child has the same opportunity to reach the highest level?

"Well, you're making them feel bad that they are only a Level 14."

That's guilt. That's not shame. That's on them. That's not on us.

This is extremely important, so get your highlighter ready. These students cannot be low-level players because the XP you are handing out is inaccessible to them. You must make sure your below-level students have the same chance to be dominant players as any kid already at grade level.

Or else, you *are* probably shaming those students.

It doesn't matter how low they come to you or how many disabilities have been identified. Every child can learn something. If a student is working hard, that student should find success in learning. Success leads to XP. Their XP leads to higher levels.

Who knows, then? Maybe by the end of the year, that Level 51 student might make it to grade level and surprise everyone.

Well…maybe not everyone.

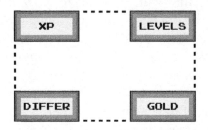

CHAPTER 9:
GOLD

Have you ever played any of the Mario games? When I was kid, I loved playing the original Mario Brothers game on the NES. Mario would side scroll his way through the Mushroom Kingdom jumping on goombas, kicking turtles, smashing bricks, and flicking fireballs from his nose. But the thing I didn't understand in the game was the purpose of coins. You run through the level collecting the coins for no apparent purpose, but boy howdy, did I still love getting them.

There is something superbly satisfying about seeing the coins on the screen disappear. You know they are now your coins, even though they are literally just code in a computer program. It wasn't until I was much older that I realized that when you collected 100 coins you would get a free life. Truth be told, that wasn't the reason I collected them. I just wanted the coins.

And your students will, too.

Gold is the Fourth Cornerstone of Gamify Education. We use gold-looking plastic coins that are each worth 50 in-game currency.

When we first started handing out these coins, we soon realized that we wished we had something less valuable that we could give to the students more often. That's why we have silver-looking coins called gold. This "white gold" is only 10 in-game currency. We soon ran into the opposite problem, though. Students were fumbling over, hoarding, and dropping these massive piles of gold and silver coins. We realized we needed a bigger-valued coin: the green St. Patrick coin worth an impressive 250 gold.

I'm not a huge fan of the green coins. There's no such thing as "green gold." To redeem myself, I bought three sacks of "solid gold coins" that make that ever-so-satisfying clank when you drop it on the desk. This solid gold coin is worth a whopping 1,000 gold.

Don't tell my wife, but those three sacks of solid gold coins probably cost an actual gold coin.

When I first started teaching, I adopted "classroom economy" as my system for classroom management. Classroom economy is the idea that students earn classroom money for behavior in the

Figure 12: *Oh, to be young again and have that much hair!*

classroom. They can also be fined and taxed money for various reasons. I created a currency called "Lamberson Bucks" with my image as the president.

Students were assigned jobs in the classroom to complete, like sharpening pencils, passing out papers and so on. Pay day happened at the end of the month. That is also when they paid their bills.

We had a market where students could bring in items to sell using Lamberson Bucks. Some students brought old toys; some made cookies and said that they were a bakery.

Good luck trying to bring in baked goods made by someone else in today's world of lawsuits, allergies, and public education.

It was a good time, but it was also a huge pain in the butt and a tremendous amount of work on my end for a mere classroom management system.

The beautiful thing about gold in our game is that it takes the best parts of the classroom economy and merges it with the other Cornerstones of Gamify Education. This extends so far beyond just managing behaviors in your classroom. And to boot, I can tell you the handling of the gold portion of The Game is far less work than needing to run my classroom economy.

****

When we were initially thinking about the components of The Game, we knew we wanted to use XP. We were going to use XP for everything. On the first day of starting The Game in the very first math lesson, I knew we made a mistake.

When I told the students they could earn a game reward in math today, participation was off the charts. Students would raise their hands, give an answer, and then I would hand them a low-value XP chip. But it didn't feel right. "If I keep this up," I thought, "the students' levels will not be a direct reflection of their learning."

That's not what we wanted, but we did want something to boost engagement and ultimately *motivational play* throughout a lesson. And that's why gold is a cornerstone.

A kid volunteers when no one will...<BOOM>...Gold
A student claps for another student...<BOOM>...Gold
A student completes a weekly reading log...you get the idea.

Before the students enter my room, I take a handful of white gold coins and stick them in my back pocket. I cannot recommend this practice to you enough. Even if you don't implement The Game into your daily classroom routine, I am telling you that you should really think about using "a pocketful of gold".

Here's the power of a cheaply-made piece of plastic. If I am about to pose a tough question, I might take out a few pieces, hold them up, and then ask my question. (I do the same for XP for really tough ones.)

Every time a student gets a piece of gold—and this happens multiple times a day for almost every student—they are getting affirmation. They are being told, "I see you. Thanks for your response." Or, "I knew you had that answer in you. Great job!" And more, "Thanks for not giving up. I'll get you to understand this, still."

If TikTok, Instagram, and YouTube get to pump dopamine into our children's brains for things that are often horrible, then we are going to do everything we can to counter that with positive reinforcement.

****

Here's another great part of having gold:

"You forgot your charger?" ...<BOOM>... "Give me gold." "You're being naughty in specials?" ...<BOOM>... "Give me gold."

There is nothing more satisfying than teaching a student the ever-applicable life lesson that if you break the rules, you pay a fine. Kids hate losing gold. It doesn't matter that the gold is worthless in society. They value it like it is real money, and for that reason, it may as well be.

Mr. Lamberson might love taking gold from his students, but you might not want to. If you belong to a school where taking away things is frowned upon, then don't do it. You don't actually need to take gold away. You could just give gold to all the non-naughty kids in specials.

If you do decide to take gold away from students, the first thing I want to tell you is to be careful.

During a professional learning event my first year of teaching, I was given an incredibly valuable analogy. The speaker said to think about your interactions with students like a bank account, filled with deposits and withdrawals. Deposits are the positive interactions with students, whether in or outside of class. These deposits could be compliments, positive observations, showing up to a sporting event, and a hundred other things. Withdrawals would be things like discipline and fussings, the moments when the student isn't exactly excited to be interacting with you. The point of the analogy was simple: don't withdraw more than you have deposited.

After fifteen years of teaching now, I think the deposit/withdrawal analogy is still powerful. However, I think it needs a little tweak as it relates to the giving and taking away of gold. Your withdrawals cannot be close to the amount of deposits that you have made. I like to think of it as 3:1. For every three deposits, you can make one withdrawal.

It feels like you're just making up numbers.

I am indeed. But I am right. If you take too much away from students, it feels punitive. The punitiveness of the system will eventually turn into that child running out of gold, Becker Bucks, or whatever currency you are using. And when that happens, the teacher and the student will have each dug their own separate holes.

"What do you do with that very difficult kid who wants to derail The Game and hinder any learning in the classroom?"

I can tell you with 100% certainty you will not motivate him by taking away all his gold and making him go into debt. Yes, he deserves to go into debt, but it won't help.

For one, his behavior may warrant more serious consequences than The Game can provide. I wouldn't even try to curb his behavior with it. I would say things like, "After we get back on track, we'll get you back in The Game. You can still earn XP and gold, but we're going to take a break until we figure this thing out."

That may or may not help. What will help, though, is consistent deposits. Whether it is game-related or not, keep pouring into that child. Keep making him feel special. Don't take away his stuff.

More likely than not, life has already taken more than enough away from him.

Mr. Becker is absolutely right. When students give me gold, they already knew that they would be fined. A fine is something a student is aware of from the get-go, something you have shared with the class, and something everyone has agreed to. So, if they break a rule on the fine list, they pay the fine.

It needs to feel fair. If it doesn't, then you're probably not doing it right. When students know they are going to get fined, they have agency in their actions. They are also more responsible for their behaviors. These are not the "withdrawals" Mr. Becker was referring to.

"What if students do something you hadn't made a fine for, but you feel like it is something they should pay gold for?"

Simple. Sit down with them. Talk to them about their choice, and why they made it. Then ask them what they think is a fair fine for their actions. Nine times out ten, they will choose a reasonable fine that won't bankrupt them.

Also, since it's their choice, you won't bankrupt your relationship with the student. This plays into one of my teaching philosophies:

Don't be a jerk.

****

"How do you keep kids from stealing these physical items, XP, and gold?"

First, you tell the kids, "If you are stealing from another student, you won't be a part of The Game." It's that simple. Your classroom game is not an inherent right that all students get to play. All students should be given the opportunity to participate, but if they can't adhere to the spirit of fair game play, they don't get to play. At first, I would suggest a "time-out" from The Game, but if you have a student who is a complete klepto, then they need a longer time away from playing it.

Additionally, I want my students to be put into situations where there are temptations to make the wrong choices when the ramifications are low. If a kid is tempted to steal their classmates' gold, what are the chances that he has the same thought when he is walking through the candy aisle at the gas station? If you never walk outside of your classroom and leave the kids unsupervised for ten seconds, how is a child ever going to internalize that true character is doing something when no one is watching?

Each class is unique with a different set of challenges. For some of the groups I have taught, all the students kept stacks of XP and gold on their desks, and nobody bothered them. Other groups wanted all their stuff kept in a bag on their desk. That's fine, too.

Keep this in mind. If a student is willing to steal from other students to be successful in The Game, then at least you know they care about playing your classroom game. This will give you a lot of power. Just make sure you use that power responsibly.

I hope at least one person got your subtle Spiderman reference.

Before we leave the chapter on gold, you probably are wondering what the students used the gold for. They spent their gold on promotion cards, wyverns, potions, shields, backpacks, owls, and as a payment for being knocked out.

That was our game. But for yours?

That's completely up to you, Gamemaster.

CHAPTER 10:
THE ALTERNATIVES

"I suppose she could just keep giving him pieces of candy."

This is what Mr. Lamberson said when he was facetiously explaining to me how a specialist might motivate one of my students.

Do you know what kid I am talking about? Do you have a completely unmotivated kid who is unwilling to try? The only thing that seems to motivate him is a piece of candy. And when that piece is done, another piece is thrown his way. If it's not, then that child is disengaged for the rest of the lesson.

We are not nutritionists or doctors, but loading up our students with candy to curb classroom behavior doesn't seem like a good idea. And this is coming from a teacher who gave away a lot of candy in years past.

Mints, specifically.

When I first started my first year of teaching in a public school back in 2013, I had a few eye-opening moments. One was the amount of standardized testing there was, but even more than that, was the pressure put on these tests—even at the fourth-grade level. Districts were compared against other districts, schools against other schools; grade levels were being compared against other grade levels, and of course, teachers against other teachers.

For someone who is highly competitive, I didn't want to look bad. Apparently, my first school didn't want to look bad either. During the state test, the school provided mints to give to the students when they were taking the assessments.

"Mints?" I thought. "That's a little weird."

The next school year, the mints were brought up again, and this time I was told there was brain research behind it. Well, after doing a little digging, the brain research was pretty much trying to train the students like Pavlov's dogs. Give them a mint when they were experiencing success throughout the year, and then when they were taking a test, give them the same mint. The students would subconsciously think they were being successful at that moment.

For those of you who don't know, Pavlov was a psychologist who ran an experiment with dogs. He would ring a bell anytime he was feeding them. At the sight of the food, the dogs would begin to drool uncontrollably. After repeating this process for a while, he began ringing the bell without the food. What happened? The dogs started salivating and drooling because they associated the sound of the bell with the meal. This 'Pavlovian' effect can be seen in all manners of creatures, including humans.

Do you remember the 90's? Oh, I do. I would argue that the sound of the 90's was this: "You got mail!". Now if you were around in the 90's, I guarantee you read that with a VERY specific male voice. This was the precursor to the endless notifications you receive on your phone, designed to trigger a Pavolivan dopamine response.

So, Mr. Becker was right. He was making his students *feel*

success, or at least an adjacent association with the emotions that come with it.

I was still a new teacher in public school. Handing out mints seemed like an idea, so I bought a ton of them. Whenever students did something exceptional during the school day, I would throw them a mint. I even coined the phrase, "Here, have a taste of success." I gave out a lot of mints to motivate my students. Did it work? Probably. Maybe. I don't really know. Did they do better on their tests because of the mints? I doubt it. If a kid can't make equivalent fractions on the state test, I'm not sure a mint is magically going to give him the correct answer.

The ingredients in mints aren't exactly healthy.

Mr. Lamberson and I purposely have not included a lot of data and studies in this book. However, here's one of the few statistics we will reference. It's from the CDC:

"Nearly 1 in 5 adolescents aged 12-18 years, and 1 in 4 young adults aged 19-34 years, are living with prediabetes…We're already seeing increased rates of type 2 diabetes and diabetes-related complications in youth and young adults, and these new findings are evidence of a growing epidemic and a tremendously worrisome threat to the future of our nation's health."[1]

Giving a piece of candy now and then isn't causing this epidemic, and I don't want you to feel bad for giving it out. Remember, the mint story? However, speaking now as a parent, I don't want my daughters' teachers giving them candy every day, especially as it relates to their behavior in school. In our house, candy is a treat, not a tool for motivation. But how many incentive programs center around candy, pizza, or Takis®?

Give them a piece of plastic gold instead. Just make sure they don't eat it.

✳✳✳✳✳✳✳✳✳✳

Positive Behavior Interventions Support (PBIS) and systems like it have swept across education in the last decade. Schools and districts are adopting these programs to help monitor and support positive behaviors through incentive-based programs.

Gamify Education's concept of *motivational play* and PBIS could not dovetail any more perfectly. Incentives work. Carrots are far superior to sticks. You just need to make sure your kids actually like carrots before you try and use it as a motivator.

You could get a kindergartener to wash your car for the promise of a pencil. But a fifth grader? You offer them a pencil to wash your car, and you'll most likely get the middle finger. Metaphorically or literally.

At one PBIS school, students could earn "bucks" for their positive behaviors. They could then cash these bucks in for prizes. One glaring problem was that the prizes were the same for everyone.

The incentives were rather insulting to older students. How powerful do you think a sticker would be to a fifth grader raised by SnapChat, Minecraft, and Grand Theft Auto?

Another problem at that PBIS school was that the distribution of bucks wasn't exactly fair. This isn't what I think. A first grader at the school actually said, "Why should I try to earn bucks? I know I am not going to earn as many as the naughty kids."

Yikes!

I did a room transformation one year in which I set up my classroom like Walmart. I called it Ten Mart. Students were able to buy real prizes with their fake money if they could do the math problems correctly. It was fun but having to buy real items proved to be way more than I thought. If each kid got just two items (which seemed a little cheap), I would be in the hole at least fifty bucks.

I hope some kid still remembers when his teacher dressed up in khakis and a blue polo shirt with a homemade name tag pinned to it. I doubt it, though, and do you want to know why?

Ten Mart was only open for 50 minutes, and then it closed for good.

What about pizza parties? Even $6 pizzas add up, and what do you have after it is all said and done? Full bellies that will last for three hours. It's going to get pricey. And if it doesn't get pricey, then the students are just going to think you are cheap.

Most incentive programs revolve around money. If you are at an affluent school with a strong PTO or you are great at fundraising, maybe you don't need a game. But for a lot of teachers out there, we don't think this is the case.

What if your store stocked game cards instead? Wouldn't students flip out if they could trade their bucks for an ultra-rare card they could use in Your Game?

It sure would beat trying to motivate your older students with all those stickers of dogs and ponies.

✳✳✳✳✳✳✳✳✳✳

Let's reiterate a major point before moving on. As stated earlier in Chapter 3, we believe there is a distinct difference between giving out a piece of candy and giving out a plastic coin for The Game. And it's not that one has sugar in it while the other does not.

The coin is associated with the play; the candy is not. To us, this changes everything. A coin is associated with an advancement in The Game and is a means to get to the end goal of winning.

The candy is… well… just a piece of sugar, high fructose corn syrup, and artificial coloring.

The true impact of XP and gold as incentives is based on the power of *motivational play*. A secondary benefit is that XP chips are not advancing the epidemic of childhood obesity and prediabetes like real chips and candy do. Additionally, a classroom game does not rely on restocking a closet with expensive items with real dollars; instead, students will work extremely hard to buy made-up items with made-up currencies for a made-up game.

No kid is going to remember how that slice of pizza tasted at their pizza party. But do you know what all your students will remember? Playing a classroom game.

Mr. Becker and The Game. Mr. Lamberson and The Game.

That's how our students remember their fifth-grade year. You already know that our former students constantly come up to us and ask us about changes to The Game, long after they are gone.

Guess what they don't say?

"Thanks for that cheap pencil that shrunk in half the first time I sharpened it."

1: Centers for Disease Control and Prevention. (2019, December 2). *1 in 5 adolescents and 1 in 4 young adults now living with Prediabetes*. Centers for Disease Control and Prevention. https://www.cdc.gov/media/releases/2019/p1202-diabetes.html

CHAPTER 11:
YOUR GAME

"If it's too complicated, I won't do it."

This was wisdom we got from a teacher who was open to the idea of a classroom game. It's a perfectly rational response to the idea of creating a game or even implementing one. We teachers already have so much on our plates; the last thing we need is another "thing".

On a cold night in the middle of winter, Mr. Becker and I sat in my shop staring at the logs in the wood stove. "What if we created a new game for other teachers to play?" I told him. "One that is incredibly simple."

We thought together, "What's the simplest mechanic of a game?"

"How about racing around in a circle? That's simple."

We went with it. We took this simple idea of racing around and created a classroom game. We call it "Racing Dragons".

In this game, students race around a track, a giant poster laminated and taped to the whiteboard. The students ride dragons which are just magnets they got to design. As students level up, they qualify to train better dragons with more speed or fire power. With their gold, they can buy new dragons and different power-up cards from the shop.

You see, once we had the idea, it didn't take that long to think of a concept since it was built on the Four Cornerstones of Gamify Education. XP, Levels, Differentiation, and Gold would all remain the same. Any teacher at any grade level could create a classroom game about racing around a circle and scoring points every time a character crossed the finish line.

We would love it if you created your own classroom game with your own flair built on one of your passions like dragons. If you do, start with something incredibly simple. Build the game on the Four Cornerstones of Gamify Education and then watch reluctant students turn into motivated scholars. Then, make sure you tell us about it. Nothing would make us happier.

But some of you have no interest in starting from scratch. That's why we are writing this chapter. We want to give you a game you can use in your own classroom. It's called *Four Guilds: The Classroom Game.*

Before we get elaborate on that, we want to share a bit of our dream. We want to create products that teachers can unwrap, unbox, and login to. We want to create games that every teacher in America could implement to transform education, so that all students can become the best versions of themselves. We would love to send you a sealed box called "Racing Dragons", and it would be ready for you to play.

That's the dream, but we are not at that point, yet. From our point of view, we have pinpointed the critical components of gamifying education and have even created some games to do this effectively. Most importantly, though, we understand the power of *motivational play*. We truly believe this is the best strategy to motivate apathetic students, and we are willing to talk to any teacher who will listen about its effectiveness.

We want you to join us in the revolution of reshaping and rethinking motivation in education. Because of that, let us introduce to you *Four Guilds: The Classroom Game.*

Figure 13: The characters in Four Guilds: The Classroom Game

Since this is an actual game, *Four Guilds* needs a rulebook. It starts on the next page. Before you turn the page, though, we want you to start envisioning the joy in the eyes and faces of your future students as they play a giant game you have set up for them.

Four Guilds:
The Classroom Game
(the simplified version)

Materials List:

* "Attack Dice": 6-sided dice with numbers or dots, one through six. (If you want students to keep the dice at their desks, have 100 dice available.)

* "Hit Dice": 8-sided blank dice. (Each student needs one of these dice.)

* Hero Cards (from Gamify.Education)

* Hero Posters (from Gamify.Education)

* Potion Cards (from Gamify.Education)

* Your XP tokens

* Your Gold pieces

* Dry erase markers

* Black or orange permanent marker

* Hard plastic card cases for the Hero Cards. (On Amazon, search for "top loader hard plastic trading card sleeves".)

Game Objective:

Whichever team has the most victories in battles at years end will be declared the winner.

Setup:

Visit Gamify.Education to download PDF versions of the Hero Cards, Hero Posters, and Potion Cards. Cut out the Hero Cards and put them into plastic cases. Create four equal stacks by separating them by color.

Before the first day of school, use test scores, behavior reports, and recommendations from previous teachers to try to create four equal teams. Assign a color (blue, green, red, and purple) to each of the teams. From this point on, each team is called a "guild". The official names of the guilds are the "Water Guild" (blue), the "Fire Guild" (red), the "Earth Guild" (green), and the "Wind Guild" (purple).

Choosing a Character:

Near the first day of school (like the second or third day), have the entire guild meet together. This will be the most important guild conversation that will shape the entire year. Explain to your students that in a few moments they will each need to choose a hero to play as.

There are eight different heroes to choose from:

Swordmaster - Knight - Archer - Mage
Berserker - Healer - Mariner - Alchemist

Note: There are 8 different characters, but 16 different avatars since there is a male and female version of each. I personally wouldn't allow two "knights" to be chosen, even if one was male and one was female. But, it's your classroom, do what you want. If you have more than 32 students, you will need to double up on a character. I would suggest allowing a male and female version of one character, not letting there be two characters that are exactly the same. But again, your classroom, your rules.

At this point, hand out the sixteen different Hero Cards for each guild. Let the students discuss/argue which hero is going to be theirs. I can't think of many better start-of-the-school-year activities that can showcase each student's demeanor and personality than the choosing of characters.

After the guild all agrees, collect the Hero Cards that were not chosen. Tell the students that they need to name their characters. At the top of the player card is a spot to write the character name.

99

Use the grid if you want to make the name look pixelated. At a later point, get each Hero Poster that corresponds to each student's choice of character. Write the name of the character on each poster. (Don't write the student's name; it's the name of the character the student came up with.) Hang each Hero Poster somewhere in the classroom for all to see. Arrange the posters by guild.

When this is done, decide how you will keep track of each character's level. You can use numbered badges or digits, a laminated tracker with a dry-erase marker, or something else that you like better. When this has been decided, you are now ready to hand out XP and gold to the students.

XP and Leveling Up

As students collect XP for finding success academically, they will turn in that XP to Level Up their characters. Remember, it takes 10x the XP to advance out of that level. Every time a student Levels Up, that character has the opportunity to become stronger. A character can become stronger in three different areas. Here's a summary of each:

Health Points (HP): The student can increase the number of health points his/her character has in battle. If the HP hits zero, the character is knocked out (KO'd). The more health points, the better.

# of Attack Dice: This is the number of attack dice a character gets to use in battle. The attack dice are the standard 6-sided dice with numbers or dots on them. During battle, the sum of these dice indicates how many health points are taken away from the foe.

# of Hit Icons: This roll determines if the attack "hits" or "misses". The damage counted up from the Attack Dice only does damage if the attack "hits", indicated by a rolling a hit icon on the 8-sided die.

When students get to the next level when Leveling Up, they get to fill in TWO SQUARES on the Hero Card and the Hero Poster. It can be all in one specific category or split up among the three options.

Milestones on the Hero Poster

When a student reaches a "milestone" on the Hero Poster, that student has earned either an Attack Die or a hit icon for the Hit Die. We strongly suggest that you have enough dice available for each student to collect and store them in a pouch or bag. This way, time isn't lost fumbling for the correct amount of dice when a battle occurs.

The student playing as E. Archer has leveled up many times already in the year. At this point, E. Archer has 21 HP as indicated on the Hero Poster and the Hero Card.

On the Hero Poster, look at the number of attack dice. E. Archer has reached the second milestone, meaning he gets to roll two attack dice each turn in battle. This is indicated on the Hero Card by two filled-in dice on the left side of the card.

On the Hero Poster, look at the number of hit icons. E. Archer has reached the third milestone, meaning his "skill" die has three hit icons on it. This is shown on the Hero Card by three filled-in triangles on the right side of the card.

If students earn an Attack Die, then simply give them a 6-sided die to store. If they earn a "hit" icon, use a permanent marker to draw a hit icon on one of the sides of the 8-sided die. If you are a crafty teacher, then create a vinyl sticker in the shape of a triangle to give out to your students to put on the 8-sided dice.

Then, the student or teacher fills in the corresponding icon on the Hero Card. The number of Attack Dice is indicated on the left and the number of Hit Icons is indicated on the right of the Hero Card.

Battles

The number of dice and the number of "hit" icons would mean nothing if the students didn't do anything with them. That's where battles come in.

We recommend that students store their Hero Cards in a hard plastic case for two reasons. The first is obvious. We want the card to last the entire year, not 47 minutes. The second is for battles. In the HP box, the students keep track of their current HP during a battle. Dry erase markers work extremely well for this.

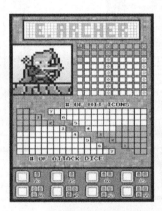

To understand how battles work, follow the progression of a mock battle between E. Archer and F. Healer:

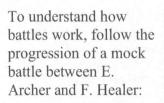

As stated earlier, E. Archer has earned two attack dice and three hit icons. F. Healer has earned three attack dice and four hit icons. It would look like this:

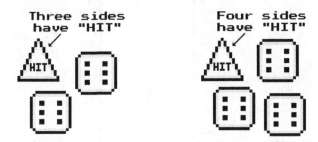

The starting HP for the archer is 21 while the starting HP for the Healer is 19. With a dry erase marker, each student writes the starting HP on the hard plastic case.

We are now ready for the battle to begin!

****

We will say the archer gets to go first. This is what he rolls:

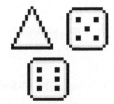

Unfortunately for the archer, the damage done is zero since his attack missed.

It's now the healer's turn. This is what she rolls:

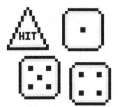

It's a HIT! The archer takes 10 damage (5 + 4 + 1). The HP changes on his Hero Card.

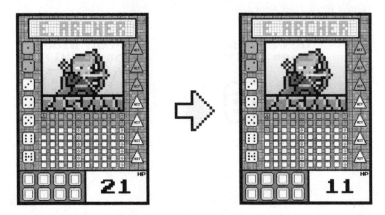

The archer rolls for his next turn. Once again, it's a miss. For the healer's next roll, she rolls a "HIT" and does 16 damage, causing the archer's HP to fall to 0. The healer wins the battle.

****

We hope you are excited right now because you can envision the fun.

Undoubtedly though, you still have a hundred questions about how this classroom game could work. Here are just a few of them:

"When do they battle?"

"How do they get matched up?"

"What happens when one of the students wins or loses?"

"What about the gold and potion cards?"

"Could I put these characters on some sort of map, and they move around?"

At this point in the book, we hope you don't expect us to answer all your questions. Remember, it is no longer The Game, but Your Game. You are the Gamemaster.

But we can give you a few suggestions.

✶✶✶✶✶✶✶✶✶✶

Q: "When do they battle?"

A: Early on in the school year, you don't need any battles. If students start at zero for all the stats, they need time to get their characters ready to battle. We would put a starting level "clause" into effect. We would tell our students that they can only start battling at Level 15. No one is going to want to watch a battle in which the students only have one "hit" icon on their 8-sided dice.

Around October, you probably would want to start at least one or two weekly battles. In November, we would announce that the students would soon need to register for the Tournament of Champions (or something like that). This tournament would be right before Winter Break. Brackets like college basketball's March Madness would be created, and the character names would make up several tiered brackets.

Q: "How do they get matched up?"

A: We think it is rather obvious to say that if you are matching students up, then the levels of the students need to be close. You don't want a Level 34 kid battling someone who is Level 7. If we were running a weekly battle, we would randomly draw a student's name. The opponent would be someone in a different guild who was closest to his/her level (either up, down, or exactly the same).

Q: "What happens when one of the students wins or loses?"

A: We would definitely do something for the winner of the battle. This could be as simple as letting them fill in two squares on the Hero Poster and Hero Card. If you do this, then students are going to get stronger in Your Game by leveling up and by finding success by playing the game.

Maybe a student earns a "star" and you put that next to the Hero Poster. The most stars at the end of the year would determine the winner. Then take a picture of the winning guild and post it in your Hall of Fame.

Maybe you are going to set something up like "Free Parking" in *Monopoly*. At the beginning of the week, every child needs to pay gold to the king or queen. Throughout the week, additional gold can be put into the "treasury" by either the teacher or the students for doing things or failing to do things. Whoever wins the weekly battle earns half (or all) of the gold in the treasury.

Q: "What about the gold and potion cards?"

A: Gold could be used for an entrance fee into the Tournament of Champions. It could be used as a payment for losing a battle. Or, if you want to get a little more complicated, you can implement potion cards that students can buy.

During battles, students can bring a potion (or two) with them. Potions enable the characters to gain back some of their HP.

Get creative if students are looking for something new. Let the students design a card that they can buy in Your Game. We will warn you, though. If you invite students to be card creators and designers, they will work incredibly hard to get their hands on them.

Q: "Could I put these characters on some sort of map, and they move around?"

A: Please do. That's what we do. Our students move on a map in Google Draw. We don't randomly assign weekly battles. Students decide when battles happen by moving next to each other on the map. It's chaotic and wonderful.

If you want to create a map, there are actual map building, web-based programs that are available for a small charge. Inkarnate is one such service. If you do create a map, don't stop there. Place a few monsters on it that can chase down your students' characters. Put some treasure chests on it that incentivizes exploration.

Soon after that, contact us to see if Gamify Education has any job openings.

****

One final note. You might be wondering what those blank dice are for at the bottom of the Hero Poster and the Hero Card. For this simplified version of *Four Guilds: The Classroom Game*, you get to decide what it is for or choose to not use them at all.

We have some exciting ideas for those dice, but we're not ready to share this idea with you...

...at least, not yet.

CHAPTER 12:
PRO TIPS

As we conclude this book, we want to leave you with some lessons we have personally learned from our experience playing a classroom game.

Pro Tip #1: Inflation needs to be part of Your Game.
Like real economies, your classroom needs to experience inflation. Unlike rising costs of gas prices and loaves of white bread, classroom inflation is actually a good thing. Without it, the energy will dwindle and the initial excitement will wane.

I'm not going to lie. I've been dying to talk about the collective masterpiece of action cinema that is the *Fast and Furious* franchise, and I think this is the perfect place. If you have been somehow living under a rock for the last two decades, it will be my pleasure to get you up to speed.

In the initial drafts of this book, references to *Fast and Furious* showed up on page 1. Somehow, by God's grace, I got the first reference to show up on page 109.

The *Fast and Furious* movies center around the world of underground car racing and one man named Dominic Toretto and his "family". The first movie is a blatant rip-off of *Point Break*, the 1990's action classic starring Patrick Swayze and Keanu Reeves, but it doesn't matter because it is still glorious. The films get more and more ridiculous and campy as the franchise progresses, only adding to the fun.

I want to talk about the racing in the first film. You see, the cars they use run on two fuel types: gasoline and nitrous oxide (NOS). The job of the gasoline is obvious. It is the primary fuel source for the car. It is what gets the car going. But NOS...oh, sweet NOS... when the driver hits that red button, the car will explode forward like a rocket.

Hopefully you can see the comparison I am drawing here. Your students are the cars, and their motivation is either gas-powered or NOS-powered. As much as Mr. Becker has tried to fight against this analogy, he knows it is perfect.

As you go about your day-to-day planning and teaching, you will assign XP for certain things. Let's say it is 15XP for getting a 4/4 on a NewsELA quiz. At first, this is going to be exciting for your kids. This is not the NOS button. This is just the first time they have had gas in their tanks, and they've been sitting in the driveway for years.

But when you have something you really want them to work for—something important either to you or something you know will be important to their future educational path—then hit the NOS, baby!

What do I mean by this? Create something for Your Game that is new and exciting and only available one time, a short burst of power to get them going. In our game, we created armor students could only earn during MAP testing. When students can gain special things, it is a signal to them that the learning is especially important. NOS!

I remember my wife, when she first started using a game in her 4th grade classroom, said that she offered a special reward for a reading test. It wasn't anything special, just a few "dollars" if they did well. She said she had never seen her group more focused or productive in the time she had had them.

But be aware, students are gas guzzlers. What fills them up and gets them going at the beginning of the year won't necessarily do it at the end.

Gamified Inflation: XP

At the beginning of the year, a little XP will go a long way. Remember, the game is brand new. For most students, they have never held that wooden hex or plastic chip. They will work extremely hard for 15 XP. Also, remember that the beginning levels don't require much XP at all. To get out of Level 1, it only requires 10 XP. To get out of Level 5, it requires 50XP, so don't go handing out hundreds of XP early on in the school year. If you do, your rate of inflation will be too high.

To make sure this doesn't happen, set some "base levels." Think of them as the average amount of XP given to the highest performing students in the class for meeting a specific task. At the beginning of the year, our base value for everyday tasks fluctuates around 15 XP. If a high-performing student passes a math quiz, they earn 15 XP. If they pass a NEWSELA article with a 4/4, they get 15XP. If they get a 3/4, they get 10 XP.

But if this would continue all year long, we hope you see the problem. By the end of the year, the students cannot be earning 15 XP for passing a math quiz. Some students will be around Level 40. To advance out of that level, it takes a whopping 400 XP. That's a lot of math quizzes that would need to be passed. Since our school operates with trimesters, so does our inflation. Around the start of second trimester, we raise the base values.

In the second trimester, we increase the base values by about 15 XP. That might not seem like a whole lot, but it can add up quickly. The power isn't actually an additional 15 XP. The power is that something changed. That's the whole point about gamified inflation. If things always stay the same, things get dull. Mr. Lamberson is way better at sensing the need for change than I am. He'll just change things on a whim. I like my changes to be more calculated.

And less fun.

By third trimester, gauge the dynamic of your room. If they would be happy with another rise in 15 XP, then do it. If they need a little more, then do that. If your school uses quarters and not trimesters, then raise the base level three times. There's no need to make this too rigid.

Gamified Inflation: Gold
Since XP is directly tied to levels and our levels are tied to the Hall of Fame, we are more stingy on XP than with gold. Give a lot of gold away.

At the beginning of the year, I give out white gold almost exclusively for in-class participation and effort. By the middle of the year, I will mix a few gold pieces in with the white gold. By the end of the year, half of the gold I give away is 50 gold pieces.

To combat the inflation devaluation of gold in your classroom, you need to do what our government cannot. Stop making more. What do I mean by this?

Divide your year into equal parts. If you already run on trimesters, semesters, or quarters, then use those time periods. Set an allotment of gold to use for that entire time period. Then, only give out that much gold. When you run out, then so does the gold. The point is if you know how much gold you get to give, then you will have a better idea of how much to give out.

"OP" is a gaming term that stands for "overpowered." This is going to sound way-too-obvious, but I will say it anyway: don't bring something into Your Game that is too powerful at the beginning of the year. You need to save that for the last month of school. If a kid feels cheated by too much luck or too much power, then that kid may lose motivation to play Your Game.

Pro Tip #2: Match the XP given out to what should have been earned.

Figure out how to get gold and XP into students' hands. Get them to feel successful. As I reflect on each year, I look at each student's level in the classroom game and think, "Is that an accurate representation of how hard he/she worked to learn this year?" If a child's level is lower than the output, then I failed at figuring out how to get XP into his hands. If it is way too high, then I failed at setting the bar correctly.

For the last two years on the last day of school, I have taken the One Chip Challenge (OCC) in front of some of my students. The OCC is one tortilla chip coated in all kinds of hellishly hot peppers. I'm talkin' ghosts and reapers. The Scoville (SHU) is the unit which measures heat in a pepper. A good Jalapeño will measure around 5,000 SHU. The one chip… over 2,000,000 SHU!

Why do I do this? Because I am a bit of a masochist and I like spicy foods. Also, one year a student asked if I would do it as she took the chip out of her backpack. I placed that piece of hell on a shelf and said, "I'll eat the chip and you can watch on the last day of school… but you have to be the better version of yourself in The Game." (To reach the better version in our game, a player had to reach Level 30 and pay 5,000 gold. No easy feat.)

I only had two students who didn't get to watch me eat the chip. When I reflected on the two students, I asked myself, "Did I do enough to get XP and gold into their hands?" The answer was yes. These were students who decided they didn't want to put in the effort. Do I love that not everyone got to

watch me down that chip? No. But I can't force them to work hard.

Flashforward to the end of the following school year. When the OCC was approaching, I began looking at the students who would get to watch me suffer and those who would not. There was one student who had significant learning disabilities. She was not going to watch me and the OCC. In my heart I knew this wasn't right. So, I made an executive decision. I upgraded her student's character. Why?

Because her failure in The Game was not on her; it was on me.

This student completely reframed my idea of differentiated learning. For some students, learning can be as simple as remembering to raise your hand before you speak. It can be keeping track of a schedule and getting to groups on time. Not all students are going to be wildly successful academically, but all students can find success in school by learning things at their individual level.

What happened with Mr. Lamberson and that OCC, you ask? It involves Mr. Lamberson sprinting to the bathroom, blacking out, stumbling, and falling twice in the hallway. We know this because he watched the security footage. The warning signs on that chip package are real. Therefore, Gamify Education in no way promotes the idea of teachers taking the One Chip Challenge.

Pro Tip #3: Figure out the length of Your Game.
You should plan for Your Game to last as long as you have your class. This might seem obvious, but if you don't plan for an ending to Your Game, it will sneak up on you. Then you won't have a satisfying conclusion to Your Game. In our game, the map begins to shrink in the final weeks of school, forcing students to cluster in the center. Additionally, there is a point where characters who are "knocked out" in battle can no longer return to the map. Don't do this until your year is

nearly over and all your testing and projects are done. Allow there to be a clear victor in Your Game. You don't need to do this, but it makes it more fun.

Pro Tip #4: Team games are better than individual games.
There are several reasons this is true, but the main reason relates to Social Emotional Learning (SEL). Too often, teachers forget the "S" in SEL and just focus on a student's emotional wellbeing. The key to SEL is balancing students' emotional needs as they navigate social situations.

Balance is everything. Balance numbers; balance skills; balance efforts; balance personalities.

I would form the teams on Day 1 or Day 2 of school, so I could start handing out XP and gold right away. But Mr. Lamberson suggests getting to know your kids for a couple of days before you place them in teams. Which leads up nicely into…

Pro Tip #5: Roll things out slowly.
You don't have to have all the details worked out before the year begins. If you follow the Four Cornerstones of Gamify Education, you can literally build the plane in the air. Sometimes, it's better this way. It will allow you to adapt to the specific personality of your classroom. Part of the fun is having everything slowly unfold for the students as the year progresses. If they knew all the prizes and twists, then it would take away the mystery and some of the fun.

Last year, my wife didn't implement her game until December. By the end of the year, her students still crushed it.

Pro Tip #6: The students will get it.
Your students will probably know more about a classroom game than you do. They were raised on XP, gold, and leveling up. Most of them will instantly understand it, and they will

help make Your Game better. Ask them how much XP they think a task should be worth. Most of the time they will give you the best answer.

Last year, I was toiling trying to figure out how much XP to reward a student when he reaches "proficient" in a skill on Khan Academy compared to reaching "mastery". A student told me without much thought, "I think 15XP when you reach proficient and 25XP when you reach mastery." I questioned him a bit. He explained his reasons, so I went with it.

Turns out, the student was right.

Pro Tip #7: Allow student autonomy in Your Game.
There are lots and lots of ways to do this. In our game we let our students choose and name their characters, but we also welcome them to suggest ways for The Game to get better. Students are constantly giving us ideas for new types of abilities, characters, cards... you name it. I even have the students help me design improvements for next year's game. The overall experience will be better when students can add to it.

Pro Tip #8: Don't be stingy.
I jokingly call myself the benevolent dictator. The primary goal of The Game is to motivate your students, but what you will find is that how you decide to run The Game influences how your students view you.

Naturally, I am much stingier than Mr. Lamberson. This wouldn't matter as much if we were playing separate classroom games, but we are not. So, when Mr. Lamberson tells me that he just awarded some insane amount of XP or bonus card, I drop my head and say, "Fine. I'll do it as well."

Pro Tip #9: Don't forget the fun.

My first two years of teaching I taught at a private school. There, I embodied the fun. We had epic Nerf fights in my classroom for brain breaks. We went on over twenty field trips. We sang and danced during grammar lessons. It was a blast.

When I moved to public school, I was scared to embrace that same type of fun. I was scared I would offend someone, scared I wouldn't be taken seriously, and scared I would mess up. For years I wasn't having much fun. And did I offend people? Yes. Was I not taken seriously by individuals for various reasons? Yep. Did I mess up? Oh, yeah.

But now, I am back to creating a classroom filled with joy. Bringing *motivational play* into my classroom hasn't made me immune to messing up and offending people. That's the nature of being human. That's what apologies are for. But one thing I refuse to apologize for is having fun.

Where's the fun?

It's in our rooms, and it can be in yours, too.

ACKNOWLEDGEMENTS

First and foremost, Mr. Lamberson and I want to thank our Savior Jesus Christ. When we think of all the "chance" occurrences that needed to happen to get us to where we are today, we are incredibly humbled knowing that he had his hand in all of this.

****

Mr. Lamberson and I were not the only teachers to make up the fifth-grade team at our school. We would be remiss if we did not mention the third Gamemaster, Mr. Jarad Skeels.

I'm not sure how excited Mr. Skeels was when I first pitched the idea of a classroom game, but to his credit, he went with it. Even when I would change the rules, add more cards, and require him to punch out more equipment, he acted like he was all-in.

He just held on tight as Mr. Lamberson and I tried to create the plane he agreed to board.

I'm not sure how many teachers in education would have done what Mr. Skeels did. I think a lot of them would have said, "No, thanks. I'm good."

For that, sir, you deserve a lot of credit, and thank you for joining us on this wild ride.

****

We both have exceptional wives who have encouraged us down the path of pursuing our dreams. They have sacrificed a lot of free time watching the kids as Mr. Lamberson and I work. They do have an added interest, though, as they someday want to travel with us for professional developments. My wife wants nothing more than to sit at the booth and sell Gamify Education T-shirts.

****

My younger brother, Andrew, deserves a lot of credit for the direction of this book. I don't think I would have ever thought about differentiation as deeply as I have without his wisdom:

"Just make sure the smartest students aren't only the most powerful characters in the game."

Additionally, our spirited arguments about extrinsic and intrinsic motivation led Mr. Lamberson and me to fully realize the importance of *motivational play*. Without these heated discussions, this book would not have been complete.

So, thank you, brother.

****

Finally, to all our students who we used as guinea pigs, we thank you. There is no greater feeling as an educator than seeing excitement and joy in the eyes of young learners. Thank you for so many ideas that we have taken, adapted, and ultimately used as foundational aspects in this book. And thank you for letting us experience with you what we loved to do when we were children ourselves...

To simply play.

APPENDIX

As promised, here is how you can set up your own XP tracker in Google Sheets or Microsoft Excel. But before you manually type in these formulas, check out Gamify.Education to see if there is a resource available that best fits your needs. If not, continue to read about how you can manually set one up yourself.

Take note of the columns and rows, or else the formulas won't match up.

FIRE GUILD

	Starting Level	Starting XP	Earned XP	New Level	New XP	GOLD
xxxx	1	0	0	1	0	
xxxx	1	0	0	1	0	
xxxx	1	0	0	1	0	
xxxx	1	0	0	1	0	
xxxx	1	0	0	1	0	
xxxx	1	0	0	1	0	
xxxx	1	0	0	1	0	
xxxx	1	0	0	1	0	

When using the XP tracker, teachers manually enter data in Columns A-D. The only formulas on the tracker are in Column F and Column G.

Here is the formula for F3:

```
=IF(SUM(C3+D3)<(B3*10),B3,IF(SUM(C3+D3)<(B3+1)*10,B3+1,IF(SUM(C3+D3)<B
3*10+(B3+1)*10,B3+1,IF(SUM(C3+D3)<B3*10+(B3+1)*10+(B3+2)*10,B3+2,IF(SU
M(C3+D3)<B3*10+(B3+1)*10+(B3+2)*10+(B3+3)*10,B3+3,IF(SUM(C3+D3)<B3*1
0+(B3+1)*10+(B3+2)*10+(B3+3)*10+(B3+4)*10,B3+4,IF(SUM(C3+D3)<B3*10+(B
3+1)*10+(B3+2)*10+(B3+3)*10+(B3+4)*10+(B3+5)*10,B3+5,IF(SUM(C3+D3)<B3*
10+(B3+1)*10+(B3+2)*10+(B3+3)*10+(B3+4)*10+(B3+5)*10+(B3+6)*10,B3+6,IF(
SUM(C3+D3)<B3*10+(B3+1)*10+(B3+2)*10+(B3+3)*10+(B3+4)*10+(B3+5)*10+(
B3+6)*10+(B3+7)*10,B3+7,IF(SUM(C3+D3)<B3*10+(B3+1)*10+(B3+2)*10+(B3+3
)*10+(B3+4)*10+(B3+5)*10+(B3+6)*10+(B3+7)*10+(B3+8)*10,B3+8,"error")))))))))
))
```

Here is the formula for G3:

```
=IF(F3<=B3,C3+D3,IF(F3-B3=1,C3+D3-B3*10,IF(F3-B3=2,C3+D3-
(B3*10+(B3+1)*10),IF(F3-B3=3,C3+D3-(B3*10+((B3+1)*10)+(B3+2)*10),IF(F3-
B3=4,C3+D3-(B3*10+(B3+1)*10+(B3+2)*10+(B3+3)*10),IF(F3-B3=5,C3+D3-
(B3*10+(B3+1)*10+(B3+2)*10+(B3+3)*10+(B3+4)*10),IF(F3-B3=6,C3+D3-
(B3*10+(B3+1)*10+(B3+2)*10+(B3+3)*10+(B3+4)*10+(B3+5)*10),IF(F3-
B3=7,C3+D3-
(B3*10+(B3+1)*10+(B3+2)*10+(B3+3)*10+(B3+4)*10+(B3+5)*10+(B3+6)*10),IF(
F3-B3=8,C3+D3-
(B3*10+(B3+1)*10+(B3+2)*10+(B3+3)*10+(B3+4)*10+(B3+5)*10+(B3+6)*10+(B3
+7)*10),IF(F3-B3=9,C3+D3-
(B3*10+(B3+1)*10+(B3+2)*10+(B3+3)*10+(B3+4)*10+(B3+5)*10+(B3+6)*10+(B3
+7)*10+(B3+8)*10),"error"))))))))))
```

These formulas might take a while to type, but the good news is that you don't have to manually come up with a new formula for F4. All you have to do is click on F3. In Google Sheets, it looks like this:

Do you see that circle in the bottom-right corner of the rectangle? If you move your cursor to that circle, your cursor will change to a "+" sign. That's what you want. Click and drag that plus sign down to F10. If you did it correctly, all the formulas should be correct for Rows 3-10. Now, do the same for G3.

That should do it.

Continue to check out
Gamify.Education for
new products to enhance
the fun in your classroom.

ABOUT THE AUTHORS

Mr. Becker is the Architect.

Mr. Lamberson is the Oracle.

Made in United States
North Haven, CT
09 October 2023